ATI TEAS Test of Essential Academic Skills

"You never fail until you stop trying" - Albert Einstein

For inquiries;
info@xmprep.com

ATI TEAS Test of Essential Academic Skills #1

Test Taking Tips

☐ Take a deep breath and relax

☐ Read directions carefully

☐ Read the questions thoroughly

☐ Make sure you understand what is being asked

☐ Go over all of the choices before you answer

☐ Paraphrase the question

☐ Eliminate the options you know are wrong

☐ Check your work

☐ Think positively and do your best

Table of Contents

TEST DIRECTION

DIRECTIONS

Read the questions carefully and then choose the ONE best answer to each question.

Be sure to allocate your time carefully so you are able to complete the entire test within the testing session. You may go back and review your answers at any time.

You may use any available space in your test booklet for scratch work.

Questions in this booklet are not actual test questions but they are the samples for commonly asked questions.

This test aims to cover all topics which may appear on the actual test. However some topics may not be covered.

Studying this booklet will be preparing you for the actual test. It will not guarantee improving your test score but it will help you pass your exam on the first attempt.

Some useful tips for answering multiple choice questions;

- Start with the questions that you can easily answer.

- Underline the keywords in the question.

- Be sure to read all the choices given.

- Watch for keywords such as NOT, always, only, all, never, completely.

- Do not forget to answer every question.

1

"Pierre and Marie's **amicable** teamwork later helped unlock the mysteries of the atom."

Referring to the sentence above, which of the following does the word "amicable" mean?

A) Chemistry
B) Competitive
C) Industrious
D) Friendly

2

"Ferdinand Magellan led the first expedition to navigate around the world in the 16th century. As a young Portuguese noble, he served the king of Portugal, but he was involved in **the quagmire of political intrigue** at court and lost the favor of the king. After being removed from service by the king of Portugal, he volunteered to serve the future Emperor Charles V of Spain."

In the passage given above, which of the following does the quagmire of political intrigue mean?

A) Political discussion
B) Political negotiation
C) Political problem
D) Political entanglement

3

"On September 20, 1518, Magellan began a voyage from Spain with five ships. More than a year later, one of the ships he used was examining the **topography** of South America in quest of a water route over the continent. However, this ship sank, but the remaining four ships explored along the southern **peninsula** of South America."

From the passage above, which of the following do the words written in bold respectively refer to?

A) physical characteristics; a body of land surrounded by water on its three sides
B) islands; border
C) coastline; coast
D) mountain range; inland

4

"A papal order of 1493 had designated that all land in the New World west of 50 degrees W **longitude** belonged to Spain and all the land located east of that line to Portugal."

Which of the following does longitude in the passage refer to?

A) It is an imaginary geographical line that stretches in a north and west direction.
B) It is an imaginary geographical line in a crosswise direction.
C) It is an imaginary geographical line that extends in a north and south direction.
D) It is an imaginary geographical line in an easterly direction.

5

"The next morning, the volcano spilled a large river of molten rock down on Herculaneum, completely burying the city and filling the dock with coagulated lava."

In the sentence given above, which of the following does the word **"coagulated"** mean?

A) Flowing

B) Liquid

C) Gas

D) Solid

6

"I've watched the ocean **lashed** by wind,"

In this line from the poem *I've Watched...*, which of the following terms does the word written in bold mean?

A) Sailed

B) Troubled

C) Whipped

D) Soothed

7

"Why do gift-givers believe that the cost of a present is closely associated with gift-recipients' feelings of appreciation? Perhaps givers think that larger (i.e., more expensive) gifts send stronger signs of thoughtfulness and consideration. Gift-giving, according to Camerer (1988) and others, depicts a symbolic ritual, whereby gift-givers try to show their positive attitudes toward the planned recipient and their eagerness to invest resources in a future relationship. With this in mind, gift-givers may be driven to spend extra money on a gift to convey a "stronger signal" to their intended recipient."

Which of the following is the purpose of the author in using the reference Camerer and others?

A) To question a motive

B) To establish a conclusion

C) To introduce a proof or an argument

D) To present an explanation

8

"Rushing to reach the bus and striving to collect everything she needed for school had left her feeling very frazzled."

Which of the following does the word "frazzled" suggest?

A) Sheri is feeling stressed.

B) Sheri is feeling enraged.

C) Sheri is feeling flustered.

D) Sheri is feeling bored.

"In several pioneering experiments, researchers have examined the response of patients who have had their corpus callosum severed through surgery."

In the sentence given above, which of the following does the word "severed" mean?

A) Examined
B) Stretched
C) Split
D) Healed

Refer to the excerpt from the script of the drama *You Can Do Wonders*:

"I will be looking, primarily, at composition for this project, so take your time arranging the bowl and fruit."

Which of the following terms below is synonymous to "primarily" in the passage?

A) Mainly
B) Eagerly
C) Strictly
D) Constantly

"The height of the shortest member of the basketball team is 5 feet 11 inches. Jaron is 6 feet 2 inches tall."

Considering the statement given above, which of the following is true?

A) Jaron is shorter than some members of the basketball team.
B) At least one basketball team member is shorter than Jaron.
C) Only the basketball team members are taller than 5 feet 11 inches.
D) Jaron is the tallest member of the basketball team.

"Next week, I have a completely bigger dinner party, an awards feast for teachers," Mr. Sugimoto said. "I could use some platters - similar to these. Are you interested in a job - as Assistant Chef?"

"Me… Assistant Chef?" Roland glanced at his star piece again. Already a dozen concepts for *hors d' oeuvres* emerged in his mind, including a design for a large apple. The title had such an unusual sound, that he couldn't help reiterating it, "Assistant Chef." He would be capable of buying his paints and have a job producing art. Who'd have believed there was an art to food preparation? "Sure, why not!"

Which of the following is the effect made by repeating "Assistant Chef" in the passage?

A) It infers that Roland doubts his abilities.

B) It indicates that Roland has not heard Mr. Sugimoto.

C) It suggests Roland thinks that the recognition is not adequate.

D) It implies that Roland likes the title.

"Five horses entered the stable, one by one. Gold entered before Colors. Black entered before Colors but after Champion. Thunder entered before Gold, but after Black."

Which of the following options reveals the name of the horse who entered fourth?

A) Colors

B) Thunder

C) Gold

D) Black

14

"The researcher was also able to devise a mathematical model that illustrates the movement and formation of these waves."

Which of the following gives the meaning of the word "devise" in the passage?

A) Create
B) Start
C) Solve
D) Imagine

15

"If it is snowing, John cannot ride his bike. If it is dark, John cannot ride his bike."

Based on the passage given above, which of the following statements is correct?

A) If John cannot ride his bike, then it must be snowing.
B) If John rides his bikes, then it is not dark or snowing.
C) If John cannot ride his bike, then it must be dark.
D) John does not have a light on his bike.

16

Angel, a college student, insists that nitrogenous bases pair randomly with one another.

Which of the following statements about nitrogenous base pairs opposes the student's belief?

A) "One fragment of a pair must be a purine and the other a pyrimidine to bridge between the two chains."
B) "The bases are linked together in pairs, a single base from one chain being hydrogen-bonded to a single base from another chain."
C) "As far as is known, the order of bases along a chain is irregular."
D) "To each sugar is connected a nitrogenous base, which can be of four various types."

Refer to an excerpt from Virginia Woolf's *Three Guineas*:

"For we have to ask ourselves, here and now, do we wish to join that procession? Above all, where is it leading us, the procession of educated men?"

Which of the following options states how the author characterizes the questions in the passage?

A) She describes the questions as momentous and pressing.

B) She characterizes the questions as argumentative and threatening.

C) She describes the questions as provocative and puzzling.

D) She characterizes the questions as weighty and unanswerable.

Firefighter Zaire is preparing a report about a recent explosion. He will include the following statements in the story.

K: I quickly treated the pedestrian for the injury.
L: The explosion caused one of the glass windows in the building to shatter.
M: After the pedestrian got treated, the Police Department was called to ask for help in evacuating the area.
N: After the explosion, I saw a pedestrian who was bleeding from the arm.

In which of the following orders should firefighter Zaire arrange the statements in his report?

A) L, M, K, N

B) K, L, N, M

C) L, N, M, K

D) L, N, K, M

19

"Nowadays, good nutrition is as close as the grocery store shelf. Nourish yourself with a regular vitamin and mineral supplement, and help yourself improve health and longevity."

As a provitamin supplement person, which of the following is the most plausible meaning of the passage above?

A) Daily intake of vitamins and minerals will have a positive impact on the health of a person.

B) Helping others indicates encouraging them to take vitamins and minerals.

C) One way that people may help themselves is by using vitamins and minerals.

D) A big help from vitamins and minerals is essential for good health.

20

Facts: A group of friends is trying to decide how to spend their afternoon. If John goes to see a movie, Anna will accompany him. But if this happens, she will be tired the next day. Dean will only go to the movies if Roland goes too. Roland will only go to the movies if John goes also. Dean ended up not going to the movies.

Conclusion: Anna was tired the following day.

From the scenario given, which of the following options is correct?

A) The facts neither prove nor disprove the conclusion.

B) The facts are in accordance with the conclusion.

C) The facts are not in accordance with the conclusion.

D) None of the above.

At Lakewood School, each new student is paired with an older student. The new students are Baron, Georgia, Sanny, and Henry. The older students are Edward, Pau, Ryan, and Wilma. Sanny and Wilma are paired. Baron is not paired with Rhian. Edward is not paired with Georgia or Baron.

Which of the following conclusions about Pau's partner is correct?

A) Georgia is Pau's partner.
B) Baron is the partner of Pau.
C) Henry is Pau's partner.
D) Edward is the partner of Pau.

Consider the passage taken from Dr. Zamenhof's *A Universal Language*:

"Learning a new language can be time-consuming, and several people will not take the time to learn one unless they have an **inclination** to learn languages or see some individual benefit in doing so."

From the sentence above, which of the following does the word written in bold mean?

A) Profit
B) Voice
C) Interest
D) Irrelevance

Consider the passage taken from the poem
Early Spring by Shonto Begay:

"Even as I stand here shivering in the
afternoon chill, just blow me, young seedlings
start their upward journey.
Insects begin to stir.
Rodents and snakes are comfortable in their
burrows.
Maybe to them, we also disappear with the
cold.
Not to be seen until spring."

Which of the following characteristics is
distinct between the last three lines of the
passage?

A) The last two lines indicate a different
   topic from the other line.
B) The past is recognized rather than the
   present.
C) The last two lines oppose the overall
   message of the poem.
D) The last two lines consider a different
   point of view.

Johansen played three instruments in the
orchestra. He played the violin for two years,
bass for three years, and cello for three years.
He has not played more than two instruments
during the same year. Johansen only played
the violin in the first year.

Which of the following shows the minimum
number of years that Johansen could have
played in the orchestra?

A) 7
B) 6
C) 5
D) 4

CONTINUE ▶

At North High School, everyone who joined the basketball camp is on the basketball team. Some students on the basketball team are also on the track team. Ahmed went to the basketball camp.

Given the passage above, which of the following statements is true?

A) Ahmed is part of the basketball team.

B) Some track team members are not part of the basketball team.

C) Some students who are members of the track team went to the basketball camp.

D) Ahmed is a basketball team member but he is not part of the track team.

"Part of this is about principles. Few will argue that space's "magnificent desolation" is not ours to despoil, just as they argue that our own planet's poles should remain pristine. Others will suggest that glutting ourselves on space's riches is not an acceptable alternative in developing more sustainable ways of earthly life.

History suggests that those will be hard lines to **hold**, and it may be difficult to persuade the public such barren environments are worth preserving."

In the passage above, the word written in bold is nearly synonymous to which of the following?

A) Grip

B) Withstand

C) Restrain

D) Maintain

27

"All of Sam's friends in the senior class voted for her for president of the school council. Some of Sam's friends decided to vote for Tony as president of the school council.

Based on the statement above, which of the following options is correct?

A) Sam has friends who are not in the senior class.
B) If Noemi is not Sam's friend, then he voted for Tony.
C) If Yani is Sam's friend, then she voted for Sam.
D) All of Sam's friends are in the senior class.

28

"In the country of Genovia, all the painters are left-handed. Every Genovian painter is near-sighted."

Considering the statement given, which of the following conclusions is true?

A) At least some right-handed Genovians are painters.
B) At least some left-handed Genovians are near-sighted.
C) Every near-sighted Genovian is a teacher.
D) Every left-handed Cordovian is a teacher.

"A large truck is parked in front of our house. The movers are bringing boxes while my parents are packing suitcases into our car. Soon, our home will be empty. But not for long; I believe that someplace parents are telling their children about a town loaded with oak trees, a place where you can buy the best milkshake in the world, a place where, if you are fortunate you might see the same people every day of your life."

In the end sentence of the passage, which of the following makes it ironic?

A) The fact that parents usually get promotions just like the father of the narrator

B) The fact that each house has its stories just like the narrator's home

C) The fact that other children are bothered about leaving just like the narrator

D) The fact that many people like their homes just like the people in the narrator's area

"Designers began to hide cameras in other objects, such as hats, books, purses, and pocket watches when people caught on to the deception. One hidden camera even looked like a typical camera but had mirrors that enabled users to take photos at a proper angle to the direction of whatever the cameraman seemed to be observing.

Based on the passage stated above, which of the following is the purpose of the camera with mirrors?

A) It allowed the photographer to take aerial images.

B) It permitted the photographer to take a photo of one view while appearing to take a picture of another.

C) It enabled the photographer to take an image with no external lens or controls.

D) It allowed the photographer to hide the camera in a hat or pocket watch.

31

"In their native environment, the koalas' senses inform them which eucalyptus trees have dangerous leaves, and they merely move on to another tree until they discover leaves that are safe to eat. But in custody, when their keepers unknowingly give them leaves **contaminated** with acid, the koalas are left with only two options: eat the harmful leaves or starve. Either option is fatal to the trapped koalas."

From the passage given above, which of the following does the word "contaminated" mean?

A) Carried
B) Poisoned
C) Polished
D) Grown

32

"Within several decades, these firms may be sufficing earthly **demands** for valuable metals, such as platinum and gold, and the precious earth elements essential for personal electronics, such as yttrium and lanthanum."

Based on the passage given, which of the following is the most suitable meaning for the word written in bold?

A) Inquiries
B) Desires
C) Claims
D) Offers

33

There are four cars parked alongside each other in a parking lot. The blue car is located on the far left. The yellow car is right next to the red car. The green car is parked between the yellow and blue cars. Miriam's car is located between the blue and red cars.

Based on the details given above, which of the following statements is correct?

A) The green car is right next to the blue car.
B) The green car is right next to the red car.
C) The color of Miriam's car is green.
D) The color of Miriam's car is yellow.

34

"I leaned against a rough brick exterior and dreamed about what I'd rather be doing. "Almost anything," I sighed **dejectedly**. I had been educated enough to read, understand, and even write some musical compositions, but I just didn't have a flair for it."

Which of the following is the meaning of the word written in bold in the passage?

A) Unhappily
B) Quietly
C) Quickly
D) Uncontrollably

"One ship left while in this passage and went back to Spain, so fewer sailors were privileged to look at that first view of the Pacific Ocean. Those who remained traversed the meridian now recognized as the International Date Line in the spring of 1521 after being on the Pacific Ocean for 98 days. During those lingering days at sea, several of Magellan's men died of hunger and illness."

Which of the following does the second sentence of the paragraph intend to convey?

A) The ships crossed the area called the International Date Line.

B) The ships passed the land mass called the International Date Line.

C) The ships traversed the imaginary circle passing through the poles now known as the International Date Line.

D) The ships crossed the imaginary line parallel to the equator also known as the International Date Line.

Facts: Catherine has a very active lifestyle and tries to keep in shape by jogging around the neighborhood every morning unless the weather is terrible, and it's snowing or raining. When this happens, she uses the treadmill she has installed in the basement. On Tuesday, Catherine jogged outside.

Conclusion: The weather was not bad on Tuesday; therefore it did not rain or snow.

Given the scenario, which of the following is correct?

A) The facts neither prove nor disprove the conclusion.

B) The facts are not in accordance with the conclusion.

C) The facts are in accordance with the conclusion.

D) None of the above.

CONTINUE ▶

Which of the following lines from Maya Angelou's *A Day Away* is a figurative expression?

A) "It can dispel rancor, transform indecision, and renew the spirit."

B) "I enter and leave public parks, libraries, the lobbies of skyscrapers, and movie houses."

C) "Once a year or so, I give myself a day away."

D) "On the eve of my day of absence, I begin to unwrap the bonds which hold me in harness."

A **chapbook** is an ancient type of popular literature printed in early modern Europe. Chapbooks were commonly small, paper-covered booklets which were produced cheaply.

According to the definition given above, which of the following statements about chapbook is true?

A) A child could easily understand it

B) It did not have more than 40 pages

C) Very cheap so that layperson could readily purchase it

D) All of the above

There are four cars parked alongside each other in a parking lot. The blue car is located on the far left. The yellow car is placed directly next to the red car. The green car is parked between the yellow and blue cars. Miriam's car is located between the blue and red cars.

Based on the details given in the passage, which of the following statements is true?

A) The green car is located right next to the blue car.

B) The green car is parked right next to the red car.

C) Miriam's car is green.

D) Miriam's car is yellow.

"In the late 19th century, "detective cameras" were popular with amateur photographers who fancied taking pictures of innocent people in the streets. The camera was ordinarily carried in plain sight. Its disguise was simple: it was a box resembling a huge, and a rather massive parcel or a piece of luggage, with no outer lenses or controls."

Detective cameras were popular with which of the following groups of people?

A) Professional photographers

B) Amateur photographers

C) Spies

D) Airplane pilots

1
1

41

42

Consider the excerpt from the book, *The Professor*:

"No man likes to admit that he has made a mistake in choosing his profession, and every man, worthy of the name, will row long against wind and tide before he allows himself to cry out, "I am baffled!" and submits to be floated passively back to land. From the first week of my residence in X - I felt my occupation irksome."

Which of the following states the primary purpose of the passage as an opening sentence to an article?

A) It intends to compare the narrator's good intentions with his malicious manner.
B) It aims to establish the perspective of the narrator on a dispute.
C) It tries to give a symbolic representation of the plight of Edward Crimsworth.
D) It aims to provide context which helps in understanding the emotional state of the narrator.

Spurious is an adjective used for something that is not true or whose authenticity is questionable.

The antonym of 'spurious' is 'authenticity.' Which of the following states why it is used in the sentence given above?

A) Because it explains the position of 'authenticity.'
B) Because it has the opposite meaning
C) Because it shows that there is some relation in the sentence
D) Because it does not provide any context

43

Three girls, Rhia, Therese and Xiera, each own a pet. The pets are a cockatoo, a rabbit, and a guinea pig. Xiera does not own the guinea pig.

Which of the following additional information is needed to determine the owner of the rabbit?

A) Xiera owns the cockatoo.
B) Therese owns the guinea pig.
C) Rhia does not own the guinea pig.
D) Rhia owns the cockatoo.

44

"Now more than 100 years old, several **delicate** paper cuttings made by Anderson are still in a museum in Denmark dedicated to his work."

In this passage above, which of the following does the word written in bold mean?

A) Old
B) Thin
C) Creative
D) Fragile

45

Which of the following is the correct written order of the sentences given below?

K: Convicted felons have very few rights in prison.
L: As a result, they have emotional and behavioral issues.
M: They cannot meddle with the general population outside.
N: Also, they are isolated in their cells.

A) K - M - N - L
B) L - M - K - N
C) K - M - L - N
D) N - K - L - M

46

"Marie Curie's feeling of **desolation** eventually started to fade when she was invited to succeed her husband as a physics professor at Sorbonne. She was the first ever woman to be awarded a professorship at the world-famous university."

In the passage above, which of the following does the feeling of desolation mean?

A) Disappointment
B) Anger
C) Misfortune
D) Wretchedness

"Various flowering plants reproduce through pollination, a process that requires outside assistance."

Which of the following options states what the author means in the passage?

A) The plants depend on pollinating factors such as water, wind, or flying creatures for reproduction.

B) Mutations that are color-related are transferred from parent to offspring.

C) Some means of pollinations are intentional, while others are not.

D) Flowering plants are the only ones that can reproduce via pollination.

Correctional officers have annual training to assure their up-to-date knowledge of advancements and procedures. They usually get several weeks or months of on-the-job training under the guidance of a more advanced correctional officer.

For their initial year, Federal correctional officers are compelled to get 200 hours of training experience. Firearm proficiency and self-defense skills are usually covered in their training, as well as instruction on institutional and safety procedures and regulations.

Based on the passage given above, which of the following must federal correctional officers do during the first year?

A) They have to get 200 hours of training experience.

B) They must memorize the inmate handbook.

C) They need to take 200 hours instruction on security issues.

D) They should take 100 hours instruction on institutional operations.

Facts: For her birthday, Jenny receives a box with flavored chocolates. Some of the chocolates are strawberry flavored, half of the chocolates are caramel, and the chocolates which are neither of those are cherry-flavored.

Conclusion: There are more strawberry flavored chocolates in the box than cherry-flavored ones.

Given the scenario, which of the following options is correct?

A) The facts do not prove or disprove the conclusion.

B) The facts are in accordance with the conclusion.

C) The facts are not in accordance with the conclusion.

D) None of the above.

Refer to the passage given below:

"John Muir departed home at an early age. He took a 1000-mile walk south to the Gulf of Mexico in 1867 and 1868. He then navigated to San Francisco. The city was too crowded and noisy for Muir, so he traveled inland for the Sierra Nevadas."

After John Muir arrived in San Francisco, which of the following actions did he do?

A) John Muir ran outside during an earthquake.

B) John Muir came up with a theory on how Yosemite was created.

C) John Muir began to write articles about the Sierra Nevadas.

D) John Muir explored again towards the Sierra Nevadas.

51

"Dressed in her sparkling high-tech wetsuit, the 31-year-old Dudzinski swam alongside me as half a dozen bottlenose dolphins glided by us like **torpedoes**. The dolphins were much bigger than I had pictured. And faster."

In the given passage, which of the following does the word written in bold suggest?

A) Intelligence and sensitivity
B) Danger
C) Power and speed
D) Fear

52

"When Joo Hyuk listens to music, he also dances. Whenever he dances, he also sings."

Which of the following can be concluded based on the information given?

A) If Joo Hyuk listens to music, he is also singing.
B) When Joo Hyuk is not listening to music, he is not dancing.
C) Joo Hyuk only sings when he is dancing.
D) When Joo Hyuk sings, he is dancing.

53

Facts: During a game involving letters, Phillip writes down only words that start with consonants, while Jeremy writes down only words that begin with vowels. At the same time, Robert writes down only words that start with the letter M.

Conclusion: Both Jeremy and Robert did not write words starting with the same letter.

Which of the following statements above is correct?

A) The facts neither prove nor disprove the conclusion.
B) The facts are not in accordance with the conclusion.
C) The facts are in accordance with the conclusion.
D) None of the above.

54

"Your duty as a restaurant greeter expects you to greet every guest politely and promptly."

Which of the following does the sentence above imply?

A) Greeters should ask what the customers would prefer to drink.
B) Greeters must grant seats to customers as soon as possible
C) Greeters should welcome the customers warmly as they arrive.
D) Greeters must immediately list the specials for the customers.

55

"Before choosing a password, however, one must identify the types of passwords needed. First, determine if all letters should be lowercase or if upper- and lowercase are both accepted. Should the password contain letters or numbers only, or are special characters allowed? What is the minimum and maximum length permitted?"

Based on the passage given, before a person chooses a password, which of the following should be done?

A) One must consider something notable from the past.

B) One must choose where to put the information to keep it safe.

C) One must determine what kind of password should be used.

D) One must change their password about every three months.

56

"The world becomes alarmingly polluted as it becomes more populated. We **deplete** more supplies, generate more waste, and cause more cumulative environmental stress than ever before."

In the passage given above, which of the following is the meaning of the word "deplete"?

A) Consume

B) Destroy

C) Own

D) Hide

57

"A one-room school has three grades: 6th, 7th, and 8th. Eight students are attending the school: Alex, Ben, Carrie, Donna, Eddy, Fia, Greg and Hana. There are either two or three students in each grade. Alex, Donna, and Fia are all in different grades. Ben and Eddy are both in the 7th grade, and Hana and Carrie are in the same grade."

Based on the passage given, which of the following options must be true?

A) There are exactly three students in the 7 th grade.

B) There are exactly two students in the 6th grade.

C) Carrie and Donna are in the same grade.

D) Fia is in the 8th grade.

"A person has only one stomach, one heart, and one brain... right? Not exactly. The cerebral cortex, the most advanced portion of the brain, might be thought as two structures, linked by strings of fibers called the corpus callosum. Each structure, or hemisphere, performs various tasks and is responsible for different functions."

Based on the passage, which of the following is the most suitable illustration of the corpus callosum's function?

A) It is similar to a computer disk used to store condensed information.

B) It is similar to a spark plug devised to ignite the fuel in a combustion motor.

C) It is similar to a fiber-optic cable used to connect telephone networks.

D) It is similar to a satellite dish designed to receive directed signals.

"Roland couldn't believe he was working on a lovely Saturday morning. He could be finishing his painting for art class, and he had an excellent view for the colors in the background. "Besides, I know nothing about catering," he thought. But his best friend Brandon needed him, and Roland needed the job to buy more art supplies."

Which of the following characteristics of Ronald is being emphasized in the last part of the passage?

A) Ronald being inconsiderate

B) Ronald's reliability

C) Ronald's confidence and determination

D) Ronald being stubborn

"The conference comes hot on the ends of the 2012 unveiling of two independent asteroid-mining firms. Planetary Resources of Washington says it will start its first prospecting telescopes in two years, while Deep Space Industries of Virginia expects to be collecting metals from asteroids by 2020. Another commercial enterprise that sprung up in 2012, Golden Spike of Colorado, will be offering voyages to the moon, including to possible lunar miners."

Which of the following is the purpose of mentioning several companies in the given passage?

A) To present proofs of the increasing interest in space mining

B) To highlight the massive profits to be gained from space mining

C) To concentrate on the various approaches to carry out space mining operations

D) To be able to note the technological advancements that make space mining plausible

Consider an excerpt from the article *Slow Death of a Cave: An onslaught of tourists threatens the pristine grandeur of Kartchner Caverns* written by Leslie Vreeland:

"Park officials have suggested that the cave is dry because of a recent drought and note that hard rains have since fallen and added moisture. Nevertheless, they have hired a paleontologist to assess the impact of tourism on the cave and to devise new ways to avert further damage. Ronal Kerbo, the National Park Service's leading expert on cave preservation, remains optimistic but warns, "Kartchner will never be pristine environment again. This is what happens when you open a cave to the public and say, 'Come on in.'"

Based on the passage, which of the following will possibly happen in the future?

A) It is possible that the state of Arizona will close Kartchner to the public in the future.

B) It is likely that additional caves will be seen near the Kartchner site in the future.

C) It is anticipated that changes will be done to save Kartchner from further destruction.

D) It is probable that in the future, the public will return Kartchner to its initial condition.

Consider the passage from the speech *The Destructive Male*:

"Society is but a reflection of man himself, untampered by woman's thought; the hard iron **rule** we feel alike in the church, the state, and the home."

Which of the following phrases is closely referred to "rule"?

A) A governing force

B) A general guideline

C) A procedural approach

D) An established habit

Consider the passage from the article *Electric Cars Deserve Second Look*:

"Furthermore, the federal government is promoting electric car usage by giving notable rebates for acquiring electric cars, and some give additional rebates."

Which of the following is the meaning of the word rebate in the given passage?

A) Awards

B) Additional guarantees

C) Tax credits

D) Money returned

Refer to the poem *The Courage That My Mother Had* written by Edna St. Vincent Millay:

"The courage that my mother had
Went with her, and is with her still:
Rock from New England quarried;
Now granite in a granite hill.

The golden brooch my mother wore
She left behind for me to wear;
I have no thing I treasure more:
Yet it is something I could spare.

Oh, if instead, she'd left to me
The thing she took into the grave! –
That courage like a rock, which she
Has no more need of, and I have."

Which of the following thoughts does the poem intend to convey?

A) To have a golden brooch is better than to have nothing.

B) Qualities such as courage are not admired, unlike jewelry.

C) Personal strengths are deemed more significant than precious objects.

D) Only a daughter can truly correlate to the perceptions of her mother.

Refer to the selection from the poem, *Wildflowers*:

"1 The iris has whorls of purple and white,
    And a stubbly beard
    That looks quite weird.

2 The Queen Anne's lace is noble and prime,
    A sovereign cloud
    Of beauty endowed."

Which of the following does the 2nd line in the passage imply?

A) The Queen Anne's lace was first grown by an English queen.

B) The Queen Anne's lace is the tallest of all the wildflowers.

C) The Queen Anne's lace is invaluable.

D) The Queen Anne's lace has a majestic beauty to it.

"The early highlights that are shown every Saturday and seldom during the week were silent films. A local, gifted pianist usually sat in the front of the stage providing a musical backdrop for the performance. Chords were beaten out as the western film star Tom Mix rode his horse up to the newest, staged train robbery or as the Keystone Cops examined another caper."

Based on the passage given above, which of the following states why a piano accompanied the sound of Tom Mix's horse?

A) Because films were silent since audio technology was not yet conceived

B) Because Tom Mix preferred piano better than violins

C) Because the viewers were producing too much noise

D) Because the music had to mask the snorting noises from the horse

Trail Safety Tips

To guarantee a safe visit, users must evaluate their limits and capabilities before starting on a trail. Public phones are stationed at the main entrance and the end of the path; however, there are no public phones located along the trail (an emergency phone operation has not been installed yet). To assure everyone's safety, please review these tips:

1. Tell your destination and trail to someone before leaving.
2. Wear clothing appropriate for the weather.
3. Bring a flashlight and wear reflective apparel before sunrise and after sunset.
4. If you are cycling, inspect equipment, wear a helmet, bring a tire pump, and keep a safe speed.
5. Be cautious around horses.

According to the trail safety tips stated above, which of the following should hikers do first?

A) Identify the location of public phones along the trail.

B) Always carry a warm jacket.

C) Notify someone else about the trail that will be used by the hiker.

D) Use caution around horses.

"The Human Resources Packet will incorporate information about the Gorman Productions Web site, other valuable Web sites, computer information, a sample production plan, and a security statement. You are expected to be familiarized with this information before the first day of work in the production studio. In this same packet, you will also find a New Team Member Orientation Evaluation Survey.

According to the passage given above, which of the following materials is included in the Human Resources Packet?

A) A Photo ID badge
B) The security statement
C) The supervisor's schedule
D) A payroll form

"Some of the biggest ocean waves in the world are almost improbable to see. Unlike other large waves, these rollers, called internal waves, do not ride the sea surface. Instead, they run underwater, unnoticeable without the aid of satellite imagery or advanced monitoring facilities. Despite their hidden nature, internal waves are fundamental parts of ocean water dynamics, transferring heat to the ocean abysses and bringing up cold water from below. And they can reach great heights - some as tall as skyscrapers."

Which of the following is the primary purpose of the passage above?

A) It serves mainly to illustrate a natural phenomenon and discuss its significance.
B) It serves mainly to note a misconception about an issue.
C) It serves mainly to present a study and review its findings.
D) It serves mainly to tell how a scientific device is utilized.

70

Refer to the excerpt from the article *Mind Over Mass Media* by Steven Pinker:

"Experience does not renew the fundamental information-processing abilities of the brain. Speed-reading programs have long insisted on doing just that, but Woody Allen rendered the verdict after he read Leo Tolstoy's famously long novel *War and Peace* in one sitting: "It was about Russia." Genuine multitasking, too, has been revealed as a myth, not just by laboratory examinations but by the familiar sight of an SUV moving between lanes as the driver makes deals on his cell phone."

Based on the passage given, which of the following does the author suggest in using the novel War and Peace?

A) It suggests that Woody Allen could not grasp the novel by speed-reading.

B) It suggests that Woody Allen did not like Tolstoy's writing technique.

C) It suggests that Woody Allen repented reading a lengthy novel.

D) It suggests that Woody Allen had become considerably skilled in multitasking.

71

"By agreement, the first assembly was confined to domestic matters. Each candidate was given eight minutes to make their opening remarks. During the rest of the hour, the candidates took turns answering questions posed by chosen reporters. Both Kennedy and Nixon dealt with the issues calmly and carefully."

Based on the passage given above, which of the following would be the possible concern to be discussed on the first session of debate between Kennedy and Nixon?

A) World nuclear disarmament

B) Trade with Europe

C) Problems of American industry

D) Politics of the Middle East

72

"In addition to performing these investigations, archaeologists have been able to examine the bones of the victims by utilizing **distilled** water to remove the volcanic ash. By strengthening the fragile bone with acrylic paint, scientists were able to analyze the skeletons and make conclusions about the habits and diet of the residents."

In the passage given above, which of the following is the meaning of the word "distilled"?

A) Sea
B) Volcanic
C) Bottled
D) Purified

73

"Minnows usually serve as primary consumers in a streambed, sometimes as bottom feeders to engulf ooze or consume algae. Others, as secondary consumers, consume zooplankton, insects, crustaceans, worms, and other minnows. Few become food for the tertiary consumers, being the target of mammals, birds, and other fish. Those of bigger sizes are used as a lure for sports fishing. Still, others are utilized as food additives in livestock feeds."

Which of the following does the word "consumer" from the above passage mean?

A) Those who serve
B) Those who occupy
C) Those who eat
D) Those who shop

74

Consider the excerpt from the article *Seining for Minnows*:

"The native behavior and skills of the falcon are valued by the falconer. The reward in working with a skilled falcon is the fellowship of a creature that can prefer at any time to disappear over the horizon forever."

Which of the following terms does the phrase "disappear over the horizon" imply in the given passage?

A) Fly extremely high
B) Return to the falconer
C) Leave the falconer
D) Go behind trees

75

"If using a metal file, always put in mind to bear down only on the forward stroke. On the return stroke, lift the file free of the surface to prevent dulling the instrument's teeth. It is only advisable to drag the file's teeth slightly on the return stroke when working on very soft metals. This method helps clean out metal scraps from the between the teeth."

Which of the following is the main purpose of this passage?

A) The passage explains how to oil a vise.
B) The passage shows how to clean a file.
C) The passage informs how to work with a hammer.
D) The passage tells how to use a file.

Consider the passage from the article *Electric Cars Deserve Second Look*:

"Furthermore, the federal government is encouraging electric car use by giving significant rebates for purchasing electric cars, and some offer additional rebates."

Which of the following is the meaning of the word rebate in the given passage?

A) Awards

B) Additional guarantees

C) Tax credits

D) Money returned

"Why do gift-givers believe that the cost of a present is closely associated with gift-recipients' feelings of appreciation? Perhaps givers think that larger (i.e., more expensive) gifts send stronger signs of thoughtfulness and consideration. Gift-giving, according to Camerer (1988) and others, depicts a symbolic ritual, whereby gift-givers try to show their positive attitudes toward the planned recipient and their eagerness to invest resources in a future relationship. With this in mind, gift-givers may be driven to spend extra money on a gift to convey a "stronger signal" to their intended recipient."

Which of the following is the purpose of the author in using the reference Camerer and others?

A) To question a motive

B) To establish a conclusion

C) To introduce evidence or an argument

D) To give an explanation

"Although the flowers of most wild plants are green or white, there are more colors now than there were 150 million years ago. Of these newer colors, yellow shades are the most common, followed by orange and red, which includes the shades of pink. Blue flowers are the rarest because nearly a few mutations produced that color."

Based on the passage given, which of the following options states why blue flowers are rare?

A) Bees and other insects avoid blue flowers.

B) Bees cannot see the color blue.

C) Blue flowers do not have carotene.

D) Only a few mutations result in blue color.

"Throughout the years, excavations of Pompeii and Herculaneum have unveiled a great deal about the volcano's behavior. By analyzing and interpreting data, much as a zoologist **dissects** an animal specimen, scientists have inferred that the eruption altered a large portion of the area's geography. For example, it turned the Sarno River from its course and elevated the level of the beach along the Bay of Naples. **Meteorologists** examining these events have also concluded that Vesuvius caused an enormous tidal wave that affected the world's climate."

The passage above narrates the after-effects of the massive eruption of Mount Vesuvius in A.D. 79. In this passage, which of the following options shows the respective meanings of the two words written in bold?

A) Studies by cutting apart; Scientists who study atmospheric conditions

B) Chart; Scientists who study animal behavior

C) Photographs; Scientists who study ash

D) Describes in detail; Scientists who study oceans

The St. Lucia Scenic Trail Association guidelines have been established to assure the participation of multiple users: walkers, hikers, runners, cyclists, and horseback riders. Remember that each user has equal claims to the trail. To guarantee these rights, please note the following **trail etiquette**:

1. Only non-motorized modes of transportation are allowed.
2. Cyclists yield to foot traffic; all users yield to horses
3. Cyclists stay on the right of the trail, except to pass; say "on your left" when passing; and move off the concrete path when stopped.
4. Have pets on leash or strap and clean up after them.
5. Carry out everything that is taken onto the trails
6. Camping is not allowed. Contact park watchman for nearest camping amenities.

Based on the rules enumerated in the passage, which of the following does the words "trail etiquette" suggest to trail users?

A) Trail users should prevent dangerous tactics.

B) Trail users should be considerate of other users.

C) Trail users should dress in proper fashion.

D) Trail users might have various options of trails.

Refer to the passage taken from Maya Angelou's *A Day Away*:

"Once a year or so I give myself a day away. On the eve of my day of absence, I begin to unwrap the bonds which hold me in harness. I inform housemates, my family and close friends that I will not be reachable for twenty-four hours; then I disengage the telephone. I turn the radio dial to an all-music station, preferably one which plays the soothing golden oldies. I sit for at least an hour in a very hot tub; then I lay out my clothes in preparation for my morning escape, and knowing that nothing will disturb me, I sleep the sleep of the just."

From the last sentence of the selection, which of the following is the most likely reason why the narrator laid out her clothes the night before her day away?

A) So that she would be able to sleep late in the morning

B) So that she would be as stylish as possible

C) So that she would not have to decide in the morning

D) So that she would not forget what she desired to wear

"In this situation, water excavated from other worlds could become the most coveted product. "In the desert, what is worth more: a kilogram of gold or a kilogram of water?" asked Kris Zacny of HoneyBee Robotics in New York. "Gold is worthless. Water will let you live."

Water ice from the poles of the moon could be delivered to astronauts and explorers on the International Space Station to be used for drinking or as a radiation defense. Breaking water into oxygen and hydrogen produces spacecraft fuel, so ice-rich asteroids could become interplanetary refueling sites."

In the passage given above, which of the following does the second paragraph support in discussing water?

A) It presents examples which are likely to support a claim given in the preceding paragraph.

B) It examines the probable results of a proposal suggested in the previous paragraph.

C) It answers a question asked in the prior paragraph.

D) It is a continuation of association which commenced in the preceding paragraph.

"The first probable explanation for "The Year Without a Summer" was suggested not until October. Friedrich Bessel, a German astronomer, reported observing thick clouds of dust in the upper atmosphere. He hypothesized that these dust particles screened parts of the earth from the warming rays of the sun. It was discovered that in April 1815, the Indonesian volcano Mount Tambora had erupted with such force that it sent an estimated 100 cubic miles of fine dust into the atmosphere. Witnesses to the eruption stated that the sky remained dark for two days. The dust then soared high into the stratosphere, where it surrounded the world for several years to come."

Based on the passage given, which of the following is the best summary of Bessel's theory in an article regarding the changes in meteorological phenomena involving Mt. Pinatubo?

A) The eruptions of Mount Tambora and Mount Pinatubo had similar effects on the global weather.

B) When the winter of 1816-1817 began, the cold weather would end.

C) The dust particles in the air blocked the warmth of the sun.

D) Mount Pinatubo caused various weather changes.

Consider the passage from the introduction of the invitation to the essay contest, *Why I'd Like to Visit Texas*:

"We extend a special invitation to enter our contest: "Why I'd Like to Visit Texas." We'll have one high school winner from each state across the country.

If you win, you will receive an all-expenses-paid trip for two to the great state of Texas! You will tour the state, stopping in six cities to visit overnight and to see landmarks. The prize includes hotel rooms, meals, round-trip transportation to and from Texas, and all your transportation within the state.

Carefully read the details below, start planning and writing, and send us your entry. We'd love to see you here in the Lone Star State!"

Which of the following options below is the most probable reason for having this passage as the introduction?

A) To instantly draw the attention of the reader.

B) To conserve space and time.

C) To satisfy the requirements of contest laws.

D) To reserve the most important information for the last.

Refer to the poem *Wildflowers* given below:

"The bellflower's cup is a five-pointed star,
Translucent and think
As an onion skin.
The beach rose smells like a citrus fruit
Acrid, yet sweet
A lemony treat.
The milkweed, in autumn, sends out its seeds,
Traveling the wind's routes
In downy parachutes.
The scarlet nasturtium is striking and bright,
A trailing vine
That loves to climb.
The forget-me-not blossom is blue and gold,
A keepsake of love
For those bereft of.
The iris has whorls of purple and white,
And a stubble beard
That looks quite weird.
The Queen Anne's lace is noble and prime,
A sovereign cloud
Of beauty endowed.
And the florist's flower is beautiful, too,
But those that grow free
Are special to me."

As the reader of the poem, which of the following can you infer about the author of the poem?

A) The house of the poet has nasturtiums encircling it.

B) Queen Anne's lace is the desired wildflower of the poet.

C) The poet knows the different types of wildflowers.

D) The poet has a garden packed with wildflowers.

"When John Muir learned about the Yosemite Valley in Sierra Nevadas, it was as if he came home. He admired the mountains, the trees, and the wildlife. He climbed the mountains and even trees during thunderstorms to get closer to the wind. He presented the theory in the late 1860s that the Yosemite Valley was created through the movement of glaciers. However, people mocked him. Not until 1930 was Muir's theory confirmed correct.

He started writing articles about the Yosemite Valley to inform readers about its beauty. His work also warned people that Yosemite was in danger from timber mining, and sheep ranching interests. In 1901, Theodore Roosevelt became the President of the United States. He was interested in conservation. So, Muir took him to Yosemite, and Roosevelt helped get legislation passed to build the Yosemite National Park in 1906."

Between which of the following years did John Muir meet the 26th President of the United States, Theodore Roosevelt?

A) 1906 and 1907

B) 1838 and 1868

C) 1901 and 1906

D) 1868 and 1901

Consider an excerpt from the story *Out of the Woods*:

"The trail led nowhere. Gabriel and Marie soon found themselves at a precipice, looking down into a canyon. Realizing that they were lost, they panicked. Every snap of a twig was a mountain lion stalking them; every twitch of a branch behind them was a bear getting ready to charge. They ran. They ran wildly, blindly into the forest ahead, slipping on pine needles, leaping over fallen branches, and looking – they later agreed, laughing – like complete idiots."

Which of the following options does the author want to tell in the third sentence of the passage?

A) Various animals made the odd noises.

B) Each strange noise that Gabriel and Marie heard was terrifying to them.

C) There were plenty of dangerous animals that were chasing Gabriel and Marie in the woodlands.

D) At first, the woods had been oddly silent, but eventually, they were loaded with deafening noises.

"Marie Curie was a female scientist born in 1867 in Warsaw, Poland, where her father was a Physics professor. At an early age, she demonstrated a brilliant mind and a **blithe** character. Her exceptional enthusiasm for learning inspired her to continue her studies after high school. However, she became **disgruntled** when she discovered that women were not allowed in the university in Warsaw. Determined to obtain a higher education, she defiantly left Poland and entered the Sorbonne, a French university, in 1891 where she earned her master's degree and doctorate in physics."

Which of the following do the two words written in bold in the passage mean?

A) Lighthearted; Annoyed

B) Humorous; Depressed

C) Strange; Worried

D) Strong; Hopeless

After listening to Marco's proverbs use, his parents said:

"Marco," his father said earnestly, "discretions is the better part of bravery."

"That's right," said his mother in her sternest voice. "Besides, this is all Greek to me!"

Both of his parents began giggling.

"Laughter is the best medicine," said Marco.

"Oh, well," said Alicia relenting. "Better to be happy than wise."

"Good one," said Marco, stunned.

Alicia smiled. "If you can't beat them, join them."

Based on the passage given above, which of the following was the reaction of Marco's family upon hearing his use of proverbs?

A) His sister was fascinated while his parents got annoyed.

B) His sister got irritated while his parents were entertained.

C) His sister was supporting while his parents were disturbed.

D) His sister was upset while his parents were surprised.

"Tom Peacock, a scientist at the Massachusetts Institute of Technology, says that understanding waves is significant to global climate modeling because these waves are associated in ocean mixing and thus the transfer of heat. Several models fail to take internal waves into account. "If we want to have more reliable climate models, we have to apprehend methods such as this," Peacock says."

Based on the passage given above, which of the following states why monitoring internal waves is significant?

A) Because the study of these waves will inform the evolution of critical scientific models.

B) Because it will enable scientists to prove the waves' maximum height.

C) Because it will allow researchers to change their focus in developing the satellite images' quality.

D) Because the study of wave patterns will let regions prevent and predict coastal damage.

"Honestly, we have more trouble with pet owners than with the pets themselves. You will notice that we have signs prominently hanging around the office requesting that owners should not release their pets from their pens or cages while in the office. Nevertheless, almost every day some owners will allow their pet to crawl or fly about the office anyway. As a volunteer pet aide, we urge you to dissuade owners from this practice. But if and when it happens, we welcome your assistance in helping to retrieve the escaped pet."

In the last sentence of the given passage, which of the following does the word "retrieve" mean?

A) Take care of the pet.
B) Catch the pet and place it back into its cage.
C) Help the pet in escaping the office.
D) Help the pet owners take care of the pet.

"Jacob has three pets: a hedgehog, which is only active at night; a dog, which is only active during the day; and a cat, which alternately sleeps for an hour and then active for an hour."

Based on the statement given above, which of the following must be true?

A) The cat and the dog will never be active concurrently.
B) The cat and the hedgehog will never be active simultaneously.
C) There will never be more than two pets that are active concurrently.
D) At alternating hours, all three animals are active.

"In articulating the masculine element, I do not want to be understood to say that all men are selfish, hard, and brutal, for most of the most excellent spirits the world has acknowledged have been equipped with manhood; but I refer to those aspects, though often noted in woman, that define what is called the stronger sex. For instance, the love of acquisition and success the very pioneers of civilization, when expended on the earth, sea, elements, fortunes, and forces of nature, are powers of destruction when utilized to defeat one man to another or to sacrifice societies to ambition."

The passage given above is trying to convey which of the following options?

A) Establishing a correlation between the spiritual world and the material world

B) Comparing good men and bad men

C) Establishing a distinction between men and masculine features

D) Comparing men and women

"Avoid physically handling any pet except as necessary. Pets who come to us are in extreme anxiety so, further handling by guests may **exacerbate** its fragile state."

Which of the following is not synonymous to the word written in bold in the passage?

A) Intensify

B) Aggravate

C) Improve

D) Worsen

"Your essay must contain at least 1,000 words, but not longer than 1,500 words. All papers that do not follow this length requirement will be automatically disqualified. Be sure that your area is rich with historical facts. Mark each fact as an endnote. Include a full biography with your entry. Deductions will be given for weak grammar and poor spelling. While we prefer typed entries, handwritten entries are allowed, but we must be able to read your handwriting."

Based on the rules stated in the passage, which of the following essays would be subjected to disqualification?

A) A handwritten essay

B) A 1,600 word-essay

C) An essay with uninteresting facts

D) An essay about Rainbow Cliffes

"Why do falconers enjoy falconry? To understand falconry, you must know the distinctive nature of the bond that develops between the falconer and the bird. The falconer treasures the wild behavior and skills of the falcon. The reward in working with a skilled falcon is the company of a creature that can prefer at any time to disappear over the horizon forever. You can join the honored culture of falconers if you have patience and admiration for wild creatures."

Which of the following sentences is the reason why modern falconers love their sport, falconry?

A) Falconry was popular among the royalty of the Middle Ages.

B) The falcon flaps its wings in an attempt to leave from the falconer.

C) Falconers like the prize from the sport.

D) Falconry enables them to work with an animal that is typically wild.

"April 1816 brought the natural spring climate to upstate New York and New England; trees sprouted and farmers prepared to plant crops. However, in May, the anticipated hot weather did not arrive. Most people continued to be optimistic, waiting for the summer that was "just around the corner." June ushered in what recent meteorologists termed as "The Year Without a Summer." In the first week of June, ten inches of snow fell on New England. Throughout the month, temperatures seldom raised above 30. Several farmers replanted crops various times, only to see them destroyed by storm, hail, and icy winds."

Based on the passage given above, which of the following is the most probable reason why farmers continued replanting crops?

A) The farmers strived in increasing crop yield to higher levels than they had ever attained before.

B) The farmers believed that the June snowfalls would provide the desired moisture.

C) The farmers assumed that the cold climate could not last all summer.

D) The farmers thought that the crops would be able to withstand the cold weather.

"These human idiosyncrasies mean we can never make entirely "rational" judgments. A new wave of behavioral economists, assisted by neuroscientists, is attempting to understand our psychology, both alone and in groups so that they can predict our decisions in the marketplace more precisely. But psychology can also help us learn why we react in disgust at economic injustice or accept a moral law as mundane which means that the nearly new science of human behavior might also describe ethics for us. Ethical economics would then arise from one of the least expected places: economists themselves.

Which of the following is the main idea of the given passage?

A) When confronted with economic injustice, people usually react with disgust

B) It is hard to predict people's ethical judgments accurately due to human idiosyncrasies.

C) The ones accountable for reforming the free market are the economists themselves.

D) Understanding human psychology may help in explaining ethics in economics.

"Although several early spy cameras were intended to be used on the ground, cameras have been hidden in the sky since the beginning of photography. In World War I, both sides recognized the strategic importance of taking aerial images of enemy territory from the newly designed airplane. To spy more carefully, without the use of aircraft, the Germans connected cameras to homing pigeons and sent them over to French army posts. Timers were set to trigger the cameras when the pigeons fly over their targets. That specific attempt proved ineffective, but the **idea** behind it did not: aerial photography became a staple of World War II.

Which of the following does the word "idea" pertain to?

A) Knowing the location of military targets
B) Utilizing cameras in wartime
C) Taking images from above
D) Taking photographs without permission

"Anthropologists define gift-giving as a positive social process, serving various political, religious and psychological functions. However, economists suggest a less favorable outlook. Gift-giving, according to Waldfogel (1993), depicts a real waste of resources. People buy presents that receivers do not choose to buy for themselves, or at least not spend enough money to buy a phenomenon (referred to as "the deadweight loss of Christmas"). To wit, givers would likely pay $100 to buy a gift that receivers would spend only $80 to buy themselves. This "deadweight loss" implies that gift-senders are not good at predicting what presents others will like. Researches have found that people often struggle to take account of others' perspectives - their insights are subject to social projection, egocentrism, and multiple attribution errors."

In the passage given above, which of the following terms is the most appropriate description for the "deadweight loss" phenomenon mentioned by social psychologists?

A) Questionable
B) Predictable
C) Unprecedented
D) Disturbing

SECTION 1 - READING

#	Answer	Topic	Subtopic	#	Answer	Topic	Subtopic	#	Answer	Topic	Subtopic	#	Answer	Topic	Subtopic
1	D	TB	S1	26	D	TB	S1	51	C	TB	S1	76	A	TB	S1
2	D	TB	S1	27	A	TB	S1	52	A	TB	S1	77	D	TB	S1
3	A	TB	S1	28	B	TB	S1	53	B	TB	S1	78	D	TB	S1
4	C	TB	S1	29	C	TB	S1	54	C	TB	S1	79	A	TB	S1
5	D	TB	S1	30	B	TB	S1	55	C	TB	S1	80	B	TB	S1
6	C	TB	S1	31	B	TB	S1	56	A	TB	S1	81	C	TB	S1
7	D	TB	S1	32	B	TB	S1	57	A	TB	S1	82	A	TB	S1
8	A	TB	S1	33	A	TB	S1	58	C	TB	S1	83	D	TB	S1
9	C	TB	S1	34	A	TB	S1	59	B	TB	S1	84	A	TB	S1
10	A	TB	S1	35	C	TB	S1	60	D	TB	S1	85	B	TB	S1
11	B	TB	S1	36	C	TB	S1	61	C	TB	S1	86	C	TB	S1
12	D	TB	S1	37	D	TB	S1	62	B	TB	S1	87	B	TB	S1
13	C	TB	S1	38	D	TB	S1	63	A	TB	S1	88	A	TB	S1
14	A	TB	S1	39	A	TB	S1	64	C	TB	S1	89	B	TB	S1
15	B	TB	S1	40	B	TB	S1	65	D	TB	S1	90	A	TB	S1
16	A	TB	S1	41	D	TB	S1	66	A	TB	S1	91	B	TB	S1
17	A	TB	S1	42	B	TB	S1	67	C	TB	S1	92	C	TB	S1
18	D	TB	S1	43	D	TB	S1	68	B	TB	S1	93	C	TB	S1
19	A	TB	S1	44	D	TB	S1	69	A	TB	S1	94	C	TB	S1
20	B	TB	S1	45	A	TB	S1	70	A	TB	S1	95	B	TB	S1
21	B	TB	S1	46	D	TB	S1	71	C	TB	S1	96	D	TB	S1
22	C	TB	S1	47	A	TB	S1	72	D	TB	S1	97	C	TB	S1
23	D	TB	S1	48	A	TB	S1	73	C	TB	S1	98	D	TB	S1
24	C	TB	S1	49	A	TB	S1	74	C	TB	S1	99	C	TB	S1
25	A	TB	S1	50	D	TB	S1	75	D	TB	S1	100	B	TB	S1

Topics & Subtopics

Code	Description	Code	Description
SB1	Reading Comprehension	TB	English Language

TEST DIRECTION

DIRECTIONS

Read the questions carefully and then choose the ONE best answer to each question.

Be sure to allocate your time carefully so you are able to complete the entire test within the testing session. You may go back and review your answers at any time.

You may use any available space in your test booklet for scratch work.

Questions in this booklet are not actual test questions but they are the samples for commonly asked questions.

This test aims to cover all topics which may appear on the actual test. However some topics may not be covered.

Studying this booklet will be preparing you for the actual test. It will not guarantee improving your test score but it will help you pass your exam on the first attempt.

Some useful tips for answering multiple choice questions;

- Start with the questions that you can easily answer.

- Underline the keywords in the question.

- Be sure to read all the choices given.

- Watch for keywords such as NOT, always, only, all, never, completely.

- Do not forget to answer every question.

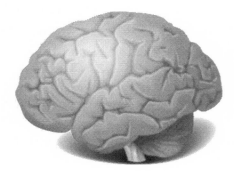

The **brain** is an organ that acts as the central nervous system. Some of its primary function are the processing of information and releasing hormones. A specific part of the brain is responsible for determining the reaction of the body to stress and acts as the sympathetic nervous system's control center.

Which of the following parts of the brain is responsible for the functions mentioned above?

A) Prefrontal cortex
B) Corpus callosum
C) Cerebellum
D) Hypothalamus

There are three distinct types of muscles in the human body; skeletal, cardiac, and smooth. Each type of muscle tissue has a unique structure and a specific role. Skeletal muscle moves bones and other structures, the Cardiac muscle contracts the heart to pump blood, the smooth muscle tissue forms organs like the stomach and changes shape to facilitate body functions.

Which of the following muscles in the human body function voluntarily?

A) Smooth
B) Cardiac
C) Sarcomere
D) Skeletal

Which of the following best describes the shared function of the nervous system and the endocrine system?

A) To regulate the communication within the body

B) To activate the reproductive glands

C) To control the balance of blood pressure and water in the body

D) To regulate the development and growth.

Which of the following is the reason why adolescents that experienced growth are physically uncoordinated?

A) Changes in the middle ear that occur late in adolescence is usually associated with the development of kinesthetic sense.

B) Fast fluctuations in metabolic processes result from the hormonal imbalances due to puberty.

C) The fast growth of the brain and the nervous system causes a lack of focus and concentration.

D) Growth rate of different parts of the musculoskeletal system are a different.

5

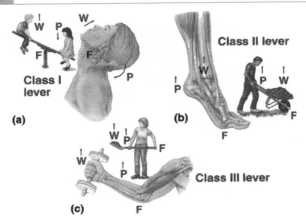

During physical training, your muscles do their job by pulling on your bones, which function as levers to create movement. First, second and third-class lever are the classifications of levers concerning physical exercises. The third-class lever is the most commonly used exercise in the body, but some use the first and second-class lever.

In the exercises shown below, which of the following involves the first-class lever?

A) Biceps curls

B) Triceps pushdown

C) Seated leg extensions

D) Push-ups

6

Body organs perform specific actions in the human body.

The discharge of liquid wastes in the body is the primary function of which organ?

A) Kidneys

B) Small Intestine

C) Skin

D) Lungs

7

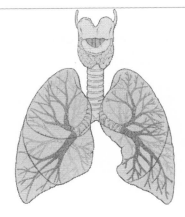

_____ pressure is required to be generated within the thoracic cavity in order for the diaphragm to contract. In this condition, the lungs would tend to

_____.

Which of the following terms correctly complete the statements given about how lungs work?

A) Negative, Expand

B) Positive, Expand

C) Positive, Contract

D) Negative, Contract

8

There are ten main systems in the human body, and each has different roles.

Which of the following system serves as the first line of defense of the body against infection?

A) Integumentary system
B) Respiratory system
C) Lymphatic system
D) Immune system

9

Which of the following elements in the hemoglobin (a protein found in red blood cells) is responsible for binding oxygen?

A) Calcium
B) Iron
C) Magnesium
D) Titanium

10

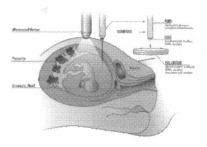

Amniocentesis is a medical procedure that involves getting a sample of the amniotic fluid, which contains cells from the fetus, and will be subjected for analysis. It is typically performed between 14 and 20 weeks.

Which of the following is amniocentesis often used?

A) For determining if there are certain disabilities present on a fetus
B) For estimating the potential of a woman to handle pregnancy to a term
C) For measuring the capability of transplant recipients in terms of immune response
D) For facilitating artificial insemination

11

Which of the following statements best describes the essential amino acids?

A) These are the amino acids considered as high-energy nutrients for promoting growth and development.

B) These are important constituents of fats, carbohydrates, and proteins.

C) These are the amino acids that occur naturally and are primarily responsible for fighting infections.

D) These are the amino acids needed for the synthesis of proteins but mostly cannot be produced by the body.

12

Which of the following order of the female reproductive parts shows the sperm's pathway towards the site of fertilization?

A) Urethra, Vagina, Fallopian tube, Uterus

B) Vagina, Cervix, Fallopian tube, Uterus

C) Vagina, Uterus, Fallopian tube, Cervix

D) Vagina, Cervix, Uterus, Fallopian tube

13

Movement is powered by skeletal muscles, which are attached to the skeleton at various sites on bones. Muscles, bones, and joints provide the principal mechanics for movement, all coordinated by the nervous system.

Which of the following about the skeletal system is not correct?

A) Osteoporosis is a disease that causes bones to become weak and brittle.

B) A tendon is a fibrous connective tissue which attaches muscle to muscle.

C) Arthritis is a disorder of the joints. It involves inflammation of one or more joints.

D) Joints are structures where two bones are attached. A ligament is the fibrous connective tissue that connects bones to other bones.

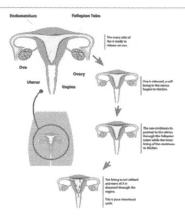

Every month, a woman's body undergoes a hormonal process, known as the **menstrual cycle**, for the preparation of a possible pregnancy.

On average, how many days does the ovulation phase of the menstrual cycle happen?

A) 7 to 10 days

B) 28 to 30 days

C) 3 to 5 days

D) 14 to 15 days

Absolute strength is the maximal force that a person can exert no matter how big or small is a person's muscle or body.

Which of the following statements about absolute strength is true?

A) Generally, women have about one third the strength of men.

B) Women can exert the same amount of strength as men.

C) Generally, women have about half the strength of men.

D) Generally, women have about two thirds the strength of men.

16

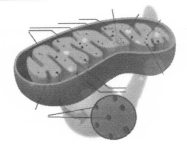

After aerobic training and resistance training, how does the density of mitochondria change?

A) After aerobic training it decreases and after resistance training it increases

B) After aerobic training it increases and after resistance training it decreases

C) For both trainings it increases

D) For both trainings it decreases

17

Alcoholic beverages are drinks that contain a considerable amount of ethanol which is considered as a depressant.

As alcohol enters the body, in which of the following body organs is it metabolized?

A) In the liver

B) In the stomach

C) In the kidneys

D) In the brain

CONTINUE ▶

18

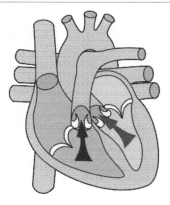

The term used to describe the amount of blood the heart pumps through the circulatory system within a minute is **cardiac output**. On the other hand, stroke volume is the amount of blood put out by the left ventricle of the heart in one contraction. In general, the stroke volume and the heart rate regulate the cardiac output.

How can cardiac output (Q) be measured?

A) The quantity of oxygen consumed times the heart's rate of pumping.

B) The quantity of oxygen consumed times the pressure exerted against the arterial walls.

C) The quantity of blood ejected with each beat times the pressure exerted against the artery walls.

D) The quantity of blood ejected with each beat times the heart's rate of pumping.

19

Which of the following is not the function of the cardiovascular system in the human body?

A) To oxygenate the blood through gas exchange.

B) To transport nutrients, gases and waste products around the body.

C) To protect the body from infection and blood loss.

D) To help the body maintain constant body temperature (thermoregulation)

CONTINUE ▶

Anabolism, constructive metabolism, is the synthesis of complex molecules in living organisms from simpler ones together with the storage of energy.

Which of the following is an example of anabolism?

A) The disintegration of proteins into amino acids

B) Disintegration of large molecules into smaller molecules

C) Forming of small molecules from large molecules

D) Forming of proteins from amino acids

By which of the following are the muscle fiber receptors at the neuromuscular junction stimulated?

A) Creatine phosphate

B) Calcium ions

C) Acetylcholine

D) Adenosine triphosphate (ATP)

The 33 individual, interlocking bones that form the spinal column is called the **vertebrae**.

Which of the following is not correct about vertebrae?

A) There are twelve thoracic vertebrae from the middle to upper back.

B) Five lunar vertebrae make up the lower back.

C) There are seven cervical vertebrae in the neck region.

D) There are five sacral vertebrae, which are fused together.

## 23

What do we call the sudden relaxation of muscle after experienceing high tension?

A) Muscle inhibition

B) Reciprocal inhibition

C) Mechanoreceptor

D) Autogenic inhibition

24

In human beings, the homeostatic regulation of body temperature involves such mechanisms as sweating when the internal temperature becomes excessive and shivering to produce heat, as well as the generation of heat through metabolic processes when the internal temperature falls too low.

Which of the following is not included in homeostatic mechanisms in the body?

A) Respiration
B) Osmoregulation
C) Excretion
D) Thermoregulation

25

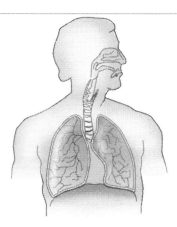

A person's number of breaths per minute is called **respiratory rate**. If a person has 25 breaths per minute, it is considered as abnormal.

Which of the following respiratory rate is considered to be normal?

A) 16 to 20 breaths per minute
B) 22 to 26 breaths per minute
C) 30 to 36 breaths per minute
D) 6 to 10 breaths per minute

26

The physical activity of low to high intensity that is dependent on the aerobic energy-generating process is called aerobic exercise. Breathing and heart rate increases during an aerobic exercise session so that blood containing oxygen is distributed to the working muscle.

What factor is increased that causes the stimulation of pumping of blood?

A) Hemoglobin
B) Cardiac output
C) Blood glucose
D) Plasma volume

27

Hormones have several functions in the human body. What is the hormone that is responsible for reducing inflammation and also known as "stress hormone"?

A) Insulin
B) Testosterone
C) Growth hormone
D) Cortisol

28

Which of the following is not defined correctly?

A) The epidermis is the thin, top layer of the skin that contains blood vessels, lymph vessels, hair follicles, and glands.

B) Sebum is an oily substance that is secreted by the sebaceous glands that help keep the skin and hair moisturized.

C) Collagen is is the most abundant protein in our bodies which gives our skin strength and elasticity.

D) Keratin is found in hair, horns, claws, hooves, and the outer layer of human skin which serves as a waterproofing protein in the skin.

SECTION 2 - SCIENCE - ANATOMY & PHYSIOLOGY

#	Answer	Topic	Subtopic		#	Answer	Topic	Subtopic		#	Answer	Topic	Subtopic		#	Answer	Topic	Subtopic
1	D	TC	S6		8	A	TC	S6		15	D	TC	S6		22	B	TC	S6
2	D	TC	S6		9	B	TC	S6		16	B	TC	S6		23	D	TC	S6
3	A	TC	S6		10	A	TC	S6		17	A	TC	S6		24	A	TC	S6
4	B	TC	S6		11	D	TC	S6		18	D	TC	S6		25	A	TC	S6
5	B	TC	S6		12	D	TC	S6		19	A	TC	S6		26	B	TC	S6
6	A	TC	S6		13	B	TC	S6		20	C	TC	S6		27	D	TC	S6
7	C	TC	S6		14	B	TC	S6		21	C	TC	S6		28	A	TC	S6

Topics & Subtopics

Code	Description		Code	Description
SC6	Anatomy & Physiology		TC	General Health

CONTINUE ▶

TEST DIRECTION

DIRECTIONS

Read the questions carefully and then choose the ONE best answer to each question.

Be sure to allocate your time carefully so you are able to complete the entire test within the testing session. You may go back and review your answers at any time.

You may use any available space in your test booklet for scratch work.

Questions in this booklet are not actual test questions but they are the samples for commonly asked questions.

This test aims to cover all topics which may appear on the actual test. However some topics may not be covered.

Studying this booklet will be preparing you for the actual test. It will not guarantee improving your test score but it will help you pass your exam on the first attempt.

Some useful tips for answering multiple choice questions;

- Start with the questions that you can easily answer.

- Underline the keywords in the question.

- Be sure to read all the choices given.

- Watch for keywords such as NOT, always, only, all, never, completely.

- Do not forget to answer every question.

1

Sean paid a total of $15 for three hotdogs after using a coupon for $6 off the entire order.

What is the regular price of 1 hotdog?

A) $4

B) $5

C) $6

D) $7

2

Caleb's bank account had a balance of -$99.58 last week. His paycheck of $282.53 was deposited this week. If there have been no other transactions, which of the following about the current account balance is true?

A) Current account balance is -$182.95

B) Current account balance is $182.95

C) Current account balance is -$382.11

D) Current account balance is $382.11

3

If the sum of two consecutive integers is 13, what is their product?

A) 13

B) 30

C) 42

D) 56

4

Points A,B and C are given in the number line above. What is the value of B - C - A?

A) -0.25

B) 0.25

C) 0.75

D) -2.75

5

A student has been asked multiply the sum of 6 and 4 and the sum of 7 and 8. The student wrote the following incorrect number sentence to solve the problem given above;

$$6 + 4 \times 7 + 8 = ?$$

How would you change the student's number sentence to correct the error?

A) $(6 + 4) \times 7 + 8 = ?$

B) $6 + 4 \times (7 + 8) = ?$

C) $(6 + 4 \times 7) + 8 = ?$

D) $(6 + 4) \times (7 + 8) = ?$

6

$$(-7)^{(a^2 - 9)} = 1$$

Given the equation above, what is the sum of the values that a can take?

A) 0

B) -3

C) 1

D) 3

7

When Alejandra divides a number by 7 the remainder is 3. Which of the following can be this number?

A) 21

B) 28

C) 32

D) 45

8

$$4 + 3x = 61$$

Which of the following statements describes the correct method for solving the equation given above?

A) Divide both sides of the equation by 3, and then add 4 to both sides.

B) Divide both sides of the equation by 3, and then subtract 65 from both sides.

C) Add 4 to both sides of the equation, and then divide both sides by 3.

D) Subtract 4 from both sides, and then divide both sides of the equation by 3.

9

6.17 x 9.7

What is the value of the multiplication given above?

A) 64.99

B) 5.9849

C) 598.49

D) 59.849

10

If 25 percent of 60 is equal to 20 percent of A, then what is A?

A) 48

B) 75

C) 90

D) 100

11

$$\frac{4}{0.01} + \frac{0.4}{0.04}$$

What is the equivalent of the expression above?

A) 110

B) 114

C) 401

D) 410

12

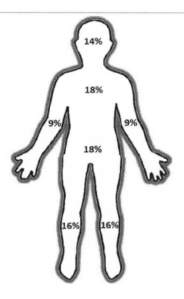

A six-year-old child got severe burns on both of his legs and his right arm during a fire.

According to the figure shown above, what percentage of the child's total surface was burned?

A) 60

B) 41

C) 32

D) 25

13

Given the equation $2(x + 3) = 8(x - 6)$, which of the following is the value of x?

A) -12

B) 4

C) -9

D) 9

14

$$14m^4 = 56m^2$$

Which of the followings are possible values of m in the expression given above?

A) 2

B) -2 and 2

C) -2 and 0 and 2

D) 4

-3, 9,-9,0

The change, in yards, in a football team's position on the field for each of their last four plays is shown above.

Which list correctly compares the changes, in yards, in the football team's position on the field?

A) -9<-3<0<9

B) -3<-9<0<9

C) 0<-9<-3<9

D) 0<-3<-9<9

	Arts	Sports	Music	Total
Male	100	60	90	250
Female	140	70	40	250
Total	240	130	130	500

Given in the table above is the number of students taking arts, sports and music classes of a summer school.

18% of the students is represented by which of the following groups?

A) Females taking Sports classes

B) Males taking Sports classes

C) Males taking Music classes

D) Students taking Art classes.

## 17

Which of the following statement does not result in a zero change in the situation?

A) Kevin earned $80 in two days and spent $80 in four days.

B) Alicia climbed 30 feet, and then descended half of that.

C) Ashley consumed 345 calories and then burned the same amount in the gym.

D) The air temperature dropped 25°F, and then rose back to its original temperature.

$$\frac{5}{9} = 0.\overline{5} \qquad \frac{1}{3} = 0.\overline{3} \qquad \frac{5}{6} = 0.8\overline{3} \qquad \frac{4}{9} = 0.\overline{4}$$

Any fraction in lowest terms can be written as a repeating decimal. If the remainders will begin to repeat after some point, then you have a **repeating decimal.**

The fractions given above were converted into decimals. How many of the calculations are correct?

A) 1

B) 2

C) 3

D) 4

CONTINUE ▶

19

$$5x - 0.6 = 4$$

What is the first step of Brian when solving the equation above for x?

A) Add 4 to both sides of the equation.
B) Add 0.6 to both sides of the equation.
C) Divide each side of the equation by 5.
D) Subtract 0.6 from both sides of the equation.

20

Bellamy decides to update his music playlist and goes on iTunes to find some new songs to buy. He ends up with 24 new songs.

If half a dozen songs cost $3, how much did he end up paying for all the new songs bought?

A) $30
B) $21
C) $6
D) $12

21

In a fire, 40% of the building burns. If the building is 600 square feet, how many square feet has not been affected by the fire?

A) 560
B) 360
C) 240
D) 40

22

$$(2^{-2} + 2^0) \cdot 5$$

What is the result of the operation given above?

A) 0.25
B) 1.25
C) 6.25
D) 20

23

$$3x^2 \cdot 2x^4 = 5x^6 \qquad \frac{x^3}{x^5} = x^{-2}$$

$$x^5 + x^5 = x^{10} \qquad \left(x^5\right)^{-2} = x^3$$

- **Product Rule:** To multiply two exponents with the same base, you keep the base and add the powers.
- **Quotient Rule:** To divide two exponents with the same base, you keep the base and subtract the powers.
- **Power Rule:** To raise a power to a power you need to multiply the exponents.

Acording to the rules for exponents, how many of the operations with exponents given above are correct?

A) 1
B) 2
C) 3
D) 4

24

Keyla took her car in for service and repairs. She had a coupon for 20% off.

Original Prices;

- Labor $244.50
- Parts $326.32
- Other $82.66

Which amount is closest to Keyla's total costs after the 20% discount and including 8% sales tax? (Assume sales tax is applied after the discount is applied.)

A) $522.78
B) $564.60
C) $653.48
D) $705.75

25

How many centimeters are in 6 meters?

A) 10
B) 60
C) 100
D) 600

26

$$0.16m + 0.4 < 10$$

Use the inequality given above to answer the question.

Which of the following set of values contains possible solutions for m?

A) {29, 43, 59}
B) {31, 47, 60}
C) {44, 54, 64}
D) {25, 40, 65}

27

Which of the following lists of numbers is arranged in ASCENDING order?

A) 5913, 5914, 5967, 5975, 5963, 5970, 5976
B) 5808, 5823, 5863, 5886, 5943, 5929, 5924
C) 5813, 5846, 5897, 5901, 5939, 5945, 5996
D) 5808, 5853, 5831, 5907, 5917, 5915, 5927

28

	Apples	Oranges
Basket 1	1	3
Basket 2	2	7
Basket 3	3	10
Basket 4	5	16

Given the list of baskets above, basket 1 to 4 contain only apples and oranges.

Which of the following baskets have the greatest percentage of oranges?

A) Basket 1
B) Basket 2
C) Basket 3
D) Basket 4

## 29

Each week, a cook purchases 12 pounds of butter. During the last month, the cook has paid as little as $23.04 and as much as $29.40 for the butter purchased in a week.

What is the difference between the highest price per pound and the lowest price per pound of butter the cook has paid during the last month?

A) $0.53
B) $2.42
C) $3.15
D) $5.17

Cashier Amanda has $146 in her cash drawer at the beginning of her shift. After her shift, there are $745 in her drawer.

How much money did she collect during her shift?

A) $881
B) $599
C) $699
D) $891

Ethan is performing an experiment in the chemistry lab. He starts with a solution that has a temperature of 24.6°C. He lowers the temperature 3 times by the same amount each time and stops the experiment when the temperature decreases to -16.28°C.

Which equation can be used to find C, the number of degrees he lowered the temperature by each time?

A) $24.6 + 3C = -16.28$
B) $16.28 + 3C = 24.6$
C) $-3C + 24.6 = -16.28$
D) $-3C - 16.28 = -24.6$

## 32

In a Research Center in Massachusetts, biologists are working on a project about DNA sequencing. In DNA sequencing, it costs approximately 20 cents to sequence 500 base pairs.

If a researcher would like to sequence a gene consisting of 60,000 base pairs, how much would it cost to obtain the sequence?

A) $12
B) $16
C) $24
D) $48

33

In 2013 Bill bought a MacBook Air for $1200. The MacBook Air in 2016 worths $780. Assuming that the value of the MacBook Air depreciates (decreases in value) linearly, what is its yearly depreciation?

A) $140

B) $210

C) $420

D) $520

34

The cost of an earbud increased from $85.00 to $114.00. What is the percentage increase of the cost of the earbud?

A) 25%

B) 29%

C) 34%

D) 74%

35

$$\frac{3}{5} + \frac{3}{4}$$

What is the result of the operation given above?

A) 0.33

B) 0.66

C) 1.35

D) 2.70

36

Malki purchased some stock on Monday morning. The price was $3.22 per share. He checked the price of the stock at the end of each day and took the following notes;

• By the end of the day on Monday, the price had doubled.
• On Tuesday the price rose $0.65
• On Wednesday, the price fell $1.24
• On Thursday, the price dropped by 20%
• On Friday, the price rose $0.26

At the end of the day on Friday, how many dollars is the price of Malki's stock per share?

A) $1.43

B) $4.94

C) $6.06

D) $7.28

37

Which of the following situations would combine to make zero change?

A) Ray spent four hours exercising this week. He also spent four hours playing games.

B) Judith took two SAT practice tests last week. She plans to take two more tests later this week.

C) Jan drives for two hours along an Interstate highway. He then drives for two hours along a county highway.

D) Joylyn walks 200 meters west to the grocery store. After buying groceries, she walks 200 meter east.

38

14, 36,...

In the sequence above, each term after the first term, 14, is six less than three times the preceding term.

What is the sum of the first four terms?

A) 138

B) 152

C) 300

D) 452

39

$$8.14 + 7.103 + 10.3475$$

What is the result of the addition given above?

A) 15.2430

B) 17.4505

C) 25.5905

D) 27.3623

40

$$5^{x+2} = \left(\left(\left(\frac{1}{7}\right)^3\right)^0\right)^{41}$$

What is the value of x that satisfies the equation given above?

A) -3

B) -2

C) -1

D) 1

41

Jewellz pays $5.73 for 0.84 of a pound of chestnut.

Based on this cost ratio, which of the following statements is true?

A) Jewellz pays a rate of $6.82 per pound of chestnut.

B) Jewellz pays a rate of $4.81 per pound of chestnut.

C) Jewellz pays a rate of $4.89 per pound of chestnut.

D) Jewellz pays a rate of $6.57 per pound of chestnut.

42

A water cooler has 2.8 gallons of water in it. Adriana spills 0.14 of a gallon of the water.

How many gallons of water is remaining in the water cooler?

A) 2.66 gallons

B) 2.76 gallons

C) 1.40 gallons

D) 2.40 gallons

43

There are 132 offenders assigned in a cellblock. 6 of the offenders are in the library, 17 offenders are working in the laundry, 29 offenders are working in the construction area and 27 offenders are working in the warehouse.

How many offenders are left in the cellblock?

A) 51

B) 53

C) 70

D) 79

44

Stephanie paid $38.24 for 15 gallons of gas. What was the price per gallon of gas?

A) $2.55

B) $2.53

C) $57.36

D) $573.6

45

	Rock	Pop	Total
Ages 16-17	22	73	95
Ages 17-18	41	44	85
Total	63	117	180

A survey was conducted in the United Kingdom regarding music preferences. Given on the table above is the data of 180 randomly selected teenagers aged 16 to 18.

According to these data, which of the following is the percent that represents those who listen to pop music?

A) 20%

B) 35%

C) 50%

D) 65%

46

Given the digits below, how many digits appear more than three times?

32901298750109384798179070775546789

A) 4

B) 5

C) 6

D) None of the above

47

Angelina placed blocks on a table in rows and columns. All the rows and columns had the same number of blocks in them and formed a square.

Which of the following could be the total number of blocks Angelina placed on the table?

A) 111

B) 123

C) 144

D) 192

48

$$\left(\frac{5}{3}\right)^{-2} = A \qquad \left(\frac{5}{4}\right)^{-2} = B$$

What is the value of $A + B$?

A) 0.7

B) 1

C) 2

D) 4.34

49

What is the remainder when 45 is divided by 8?

A) 2

B) 3

C) 5

D) 8

50

$$\frac{3}{5}$$

What is the percentage of the fraction given above?

A) 20%

B) 30%

C) 40%

D) 60%

51

A ceiling fan can rotate 75 times per minute. The fan rotated a total of 22,500 times. How many hours did the fan rotate?

A) The fan rotated for 0.5 hours.

B) The fan rotated for 3 hours.

C) The fan rotated for 5 hours.

D) The fan rotated for 300 hours.

52

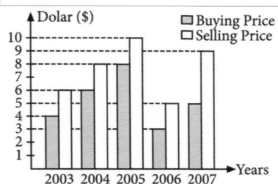

The column chart given above shows the buying and selling prices of items sold in a store between 2003 and 2007.

How many percents is the profit margin of the store in 2007?

A) 40

B) 50

C) 80

D) 90

CONTINUE ▶

53

$$\frac{5}{8} = 0.625 \qquad \frac{3}{8} = 0.375 \qquad \frac{5}{11} = 0.45 \qquad \frac{4}{25} = 0.16$$

Any fraction in lowest terms can be written as either a terminating decimal. If you end up with a remainder of 0, then you have a **terminating decimal**.

The fractions given above were converted into decimals. How many of the calculations are correct?

A) 1

B) 2

C) 3

D) 4

54

What digit is in the hundredths place of the number 7,231.5697?

A) 2

B) 3

C) 6

D) 9

55

$$4 \cdot 11 + 2 \cdot 5 - 3 \cdot 12$$

What is the result of the operation given above?

A) 18

B) 576

C) 654

D) 1,248

56

There are D dogs that live in Nicole's neighborhood. There are 3 times as many cats, C, that live in her neighborhood as dogs.

If there are 18 cats in Nicole's neighborhood, which of the following statements about this situation is true?

A) The situation can be represented by the equation $3D = C$; therefore, since there are 18 cats there are also 54 dogs.

B) The situation can be represented by the equation $3D = C$; therefore, since there are 18 cats there are also 6 dogs.

C) The situation can be represented by the equation $3C = D$; therefore, since there are 18 cats there are also 54 dogs.

D) The situation can be represented by the equation $3C = D$; therefore, since there are 18 cats there are also 6 dogs.

57

How long does it take to drive a specific route if the driver starts at 9:50 A.M. to 2:05 P.M. to complete the given path?

A) 4 hours and 15 minutes
B) 4 hours and 35 minutes
C) 5 hours and 15 minutes
D) 6 hours and 25 minutes

58

A special 35% off for one-day will be offered by Macys. Sera, a buyer, has an extra 10% off.

If Sera is going to buy $120 worth item, what would be her final bill if the extra 10% is applied aside from the one-day special discount?

A) 66
B) 70.2
C) 72
D) 78

59

In Ms. Sapinski's history class in Nutley High School, the ratio of boys to girls is 2:5. The class sizes at Nutley High School range from 16 to 25 students per class.

What is the total number of students in Ms. Sapinski's class?

A) 18 students
B) 20 students
C) 21 students
D) 24 students

60

A corrections officer receives $42,858 annually. How much is his average weekly pay?

A) $824
B) $893
C) $1,190
D) $3,571

61

$$\frac{3^5 + 3^6 + 3^7}{3^3 + 3^4 + 3^5}$$

What is the value of expression given above?

A) 3
B) 9
C) 27
D) 81

62

Which situation can be represented by the equation A=7B?

A) Aila earned $7 for babysitting. He also earned B dollars for mowing lawns. Aila earned a total of A dollars for mowing lawns and babysitting.

B) Aila correctly answered B questions on a quiz. Each question was A points. Aila received a total of 7 points on the quiz.

C) Aila baked A batches of cookies. There were 7 cookies in each batch. Aila baked a total of B cookies.

D) Aila bought B items at a store. Each item costs $7. Aila spent a total of A dollars at the store.

63

$$5x - 2x - x = 11 - 2 + 15$$

Given the equation, which of the following is the value of x?

A) 20.86
B) 12
C) 18.79
D) 73

64

PITI refers to a mortgage payment which is the total of monthly principal, interest, taxes, and insurance.

Which of the following would a borrower with a weekly income of $2,150 qualify for a maximum monthly PITI payment under the 28% housing ratio guideline?

A) $2,312.19
B) $2,512.35
C) $2,608.67
D) $2,408.00

65

A parcel of property having an area of 2,356,000 square feet has a width of 3100 feet.

How deep is the property?

A) 760 feet

B) 2350 feet

C) 3100 feet

D) 6000 feet

66

How many pairs of numbers below are EXACTLY THE SAME?

545206581 – 545206581
275330968 – 275330968
892611899 – 892611894
147238117 – 147235117
821456849 – 821456849
651942565 – 651942565
972962749 – 972967249
350700517 – 350700517
497228991 – 497228991
213864748 – 213864748
655301147 – 655301147
980463326 – 980463362

A) Eight pairs

B) Nine pairs

C) Ten pairs

D) Eleven pairs

67

Last year, Annemarie had 50 model airplanes in her collection. This year she has 32% more model airplanes. Annemarie then gave her brother, Joseph 12 model airplanes to start a collection.

How many model airplanes does Annemarie have after she gave 12 to her brother?

A) 36

B) 54

C) 86

D) 102

68

The current temperature is –13°C. The high temperature yesterday was as many degrees above 0°C as the current temperature is below 0°C.

Which of the following expressions could be used to find the number of degrees between the current temperature and yesterday's high temperature?

A) –13+13

B) 0–13

C) 13+13

D) 13+0

69

Manuela is buying items at a store. Her total comes to $64.96. She uses all of the money that is still on a gift card to pay for part of the total. She pays the remaining $21.18 with cash.

Which percentage of the total did Manuela pay for with the gift card?

A) 25%

B) 33%

C) 48%

D) 67%

70

Brian used 5 gallons of paint to cover 6,375 square feet of a wall.

At this same rate, what is the total area of the wall, in square feet, that Phil will cover using 7 gallons of paint?

A) 5,625 square feet

B) 6,375 square feet

C) 8,925 square feet

D) 15,600 square feet

71

$$2m3m+m45=3683$$

If m is a non-zero digit in the numbers given above, what is the value of m?

A) 2

B) 3

C) 6

D) 8

72

Leah went to a nutritionist and was advised to keep her food intake at 2000 calories a day. During the weekend, she attended a wedding and ate more than her daily recommended intake. At the end of the week, the number of calories she consumed was at 14400.

How many extra calories did she take from the wedding food?

A) 780

B) 550

C) 270

D) 400

73

Each day of the month, Chad earns an allowance, in cents, equal to the square of that date of the month.

Which of the following can be the number of cents Chad could earn in a single day?

A) 23

B) 35

C) 49

D) 76

74

During an 8-week diet program Lucas lost 12 pounds. The amount Lucas lost in the second 4-week period of his diet is half the amount he lost in the first 4-week period. So, how many pounds did Lucas lose in the first 4-week period?

A) 3 pounds

B) 4 pounds

C) 6 pounds

D) 8 pounds

75

When Stephen started hiking at sea level he recorded his starting position as 0. Then he climbed upward, and his elevation increased by 500 feet. He recorded his ending position as 500. Using this same method of measuring, a second hiker had a starting position of –40.

Which statement describes the starting position of the second hiker?

A) The second hiker started 40 feet above sea level.

B) The second hiker started 40 feet above the ending position of Stephen.

C) The second hiker started 40 feet below sea level.

D) The second hiker started 40 feet below the ending position of Stephen.

76

$$\frac{4^x}{2^x + 2^x} = 32$$

What is the value of x which satisfies the equation given above?

A) 2

B) 4

C) 6

D) 8

77

Working together, Kayla and Jane tiled a total of 240 square feet in 3 hours. They each tiled the same number of square feet.

What is the average rate that Kayla and Jane each tiled in square feet per hour?

A) 40 square feet per hour

B) 60 square feet per hour

C) 80 square feet per hour

D) 360 square feet per hour

78

The start of a play is represented by the number 0. Elleny arrived 12 minutes before the play started. The time she arrived is represented by the number −12. Nasai arrived 11 minutes after the play started. The number that represents the time Danielle arrived at the play is −14.

At what point did Danielle arrive at the play?

A) Before Elleny

B) After Nasai

C) After the play started and before Nasai

D) After Elleny and before the play started

79

$$4x + 3y = 19.25 = 2x + 7y$$

In the equation given above, what is the value of $x + y$?

A) 0.75

B) 3.5

C) 4.75

D) 5.25

80

A transportation company carries the packages to a specific destination. The company charges $80 for the first 5kg and $10 for each additional 3kg or part thereof.

What would be the weight of the package for which the charge is $150?

A) 21

B) 25.8

C) 26.2

D) 35

81

When the positive integer m is divided by 5, the remainder is 3. What is the remainder if 4 m is divided by 5?

A) 1
B) 2
C) 3
D) 4

82

The length of one piece of pipe is 6 inches more than three times the length of a shorter section. If the length of the longer pipe is 33 inches, what is the length, in inches, of the shorter pipe?

A) 9
B) 10
C) 11
D) 13

83

Jeel pays $140 for a yearly membership to a club and pays $5 for each visit. What is the total number of visits if Jeel's total bill is $180?

A) 8
B) 28
C) 32
D) 36

84

Michael leaves his house and bikes south at a constant speed of 8 miles per hour. His dad, John, leaves the same house three hours later, driving south at a constant speed of 12 miles per hour.

How long will it take for dad, John, in hours, to reach the son, Michael?

A) 2
B) 3
C) 4
D) 6

85

Gasoline Used and Miles Driven

Type of Car	Gallons of Gasoline Used	Miles Driven
A	4	140
B	8	220
C	16	320
D	20	400

The table given above shows the numbers of gallons of gasoline used and the miles driven for different types of cars.

Which type of car had the highest number of miles per gallon?

A) Type D

B) Type C

C) Type B

D) Type A

86

The total cost of 7 pens and 3 pencils is $47. The cost of 4 pencils and 5 pens is $41. How many dollars will it cost to buy 2 pens and 6 pencils?

A) 24

B) 34

C) 38

D) 40

87

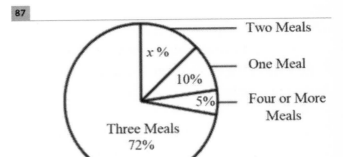

Given on the graph above is the results of the survey onducted to know how many meals college students typically eat per day.

How many students reported they typically eat two meals per day if 1200 students responded to the survey?

A) 60

B) 120

C) 156

D) 180

88

The price of an antique increased by 20% but is then decreased by 20%.

Which of the following is the overall change of initial price in terms of percent?

A) No change

B) Reduced by 20%

C) Raised by 4%

D) Reduced by 4%

89

A property originally purchased a year ago for $1,750,000 is now valued at $2,080,000. What is the percentage rate of appreciation?

Note: round to the nearest tenth by rounding up five and above and rounding down four and below.

A) 8.4%

B) 17.5%

C) 18.9%

D) 84.0%

90

A commission of $18,975 was received by a broker for selling a property priced at $345,000.

What was the broker's commission rate?

A) 5.0%

B) 5.5%

C) 6.0%

D) 6.5%

91

A property initially purchased for $1,000,000 increased in value by 7% per year for three years.

Which of the following was the value of the property after the third year?

A) $1,230,000

B) $1,225,043

C) $1,210,000

D) $1,200,000

92

Type of chese	Weight (g)	Percentage (%)
Mozzarella	850	
Cheddar	300	15
Gouda	250	
Parmesan		

Maggie wants to buy different types of cheeses. Given above is the list of cheese she bought online.

How many grams of parmesan did she buy?

A) 100

B) 500

C) 600

D) 1400

The bottom of a swimming pool is 8 feet below the surface of the water in the pool. The surface of the water is represented by the number 0, and the bottom of the pool is represented by the number −8. The pool's diving board is the same distance above the surface of the water as the bottom of the pool is below the surface of the water.

What number represents the location of the diving board?

A) 8

B) 0

C) 16

D) -8

A facility spends an average of $42,000 annually for each of its 512 inmates. How much quarterly budget should be allocated for this facility?

A) $5.37 million

B) $10.74 million

C) $21.5 million

D) $82 million

Bryan, an employee at a manufacturing company, gets paid $10.00 an hour for regular work and 1.5 times the hourly rate for each hour of overtime work.

How much should Bryan be paid if he works 40 regular hours and 4 overtime hours?

A) $640

B) $460

C) $560

D) $650

For safety, firefighter wants to place the base of the ladder at a distance equal to 20% of its length away from the base of a building.

If the ladder is 60 feet tall, how far away from the base of the building should he place the ladder?

A) 24 feet

B) 20 feet

C) 12 feet

D) 10 feet

CONTINUE ▶

Three friends went out to celebrate one of them getting a promotion. Jasmine orders a bottle of water for $2.25, Matt orders a bottle of wine for $10.25, while John orders a cocktail for $8.50.

If they split the bill equally between the three, how much does each of them has to pay?

A) $7

B) $6.9

C) $8.2

D) $8

$$23 - (3x + 2) = 2(x + 9) + 5x$$

Given the equation, which of the following is the value of x?

A) 0.3

B) 3.8

C) 4.1

D) 0.8

Esra's Cupcake Factory makes the best cupcakes by using four ingredients. For the special cupcake, they use;

- 3 blueberries for every strawberry,
- 4 raspberries for every blueberry and
- 2 pineapple for every strawberry.

If they use 12 blueberries, how many pieces of fruits do they use?

A) 12

B) 24

C) 48

D) 72

Chelsey and Harper looked up some hotels in Amsterdam for their weekend trip the following month. The one they decide on has queen bedrooms and twin bedrooms. There are 2100 rooms in the hotel, and the number of twin bedrooms is half the number of queen bedrooms.

How many twin bedrooms are there in the hotel they have picked?

A) 700

B) 1000

C) 1500

D) 900

CONTINUE ▶

SECTION 3 - MATH - NUMBER SENSE & BASIC ALGEBRA

#	Answer	Topic	Subtopic	#	Answer	Topic	Subtopic	#	Answer	Topic	Subtopic	#	Answer	Topic	Subtopic
1	D	TB	S1	26	A	TB	S1	51	C	TB	S1	76	C	TB	S1
2	B	TB	S1	27	C	TB	S1	52	C	TB	S1	77	A	TB	S1
3	C	TB	S1	28	B	TB	S1	53	C	TB	S1	78	A	TB	S1
4	C	TB	S1	29	D	TB	S1	54	D	TB	S1	79	D	TB	S1
5	D	TB	S1	30	B	TB	S1	55	A	TB	S1	80	B	TB	S1
6	A	TB	S1	31	A	TB	S1	56	B	TB	S1	81	B	TB	S1
7	C	TB	S1	32	C	TB	S1	57	A	TB	S1	82	A	TB	S1
8	D	TB	S1	33	A	TB	S1	58	B	TB	S1	83	A	TB	S1
9	D	TB	S1	34	B	TB	S1	59	C	TB	S1	84	D	TB	S1
10	B	TB	S1	35	C	TB	S1	60	A	TB	S1	85	D	TB	S1
11	D	TB	S1	36	B	TB	S1	61	B	TB	S1	86	B	TB	S1
12	B	TB	S1	37	D	TB	S1	62	D	TB	S1	87	C	TB	S1
13	D	TB	S1	38	D	TB	S1	63	B	TB	S1	88	C	TB	S1
14	C	TB	S1	39	C	TB	S1	64	C	TB	S1	89	C	TB	S1
15	A	TB	S1	40	B	TB	S1	65	A	TB	S1	90	B	TB	S1
16	C	TB	S1	41	A	TB	S1	66	A	TB	S1	91	B	TB	S1
17	B	TB	S1	42	A	TB	S1	67	B	TB	S1	92	C	TB	S1
18	C	TB	S1	43	B	TB	S1	68	C	TB	S1	93	A	TB	S1
19	B	TB	S1	44	B	TB	S1	69	D	TB	S1	94	A	TB	S1
20	D	TB	S1	45	D	TB	S1	70	C	TB	S1	95	B	TB	S1
21	B	TB	S1	46	C	TB	S1	71	D	TB	S1	96	C	TB	S1
22	C	TB	S1	47	C	TB	S1	72	D	TB	S1	97	A	TB	S1
23	A	TB	S1	48	B	TB	S1	73	C	TB	S1	98	A	TB	S1
24	B	TB	S1	49	C	TB	S1	74	D	TB	S1	99	D	TB	S1
25	A	TB	S1	50	D	TB	S1	75	C	TB	S1	100	A	TB	S1

Topics & Subtopics

Code	Description	Code	Description
SB1	Number Sense and Basic Algebra	TB	Mathematics

CONTINUE ▶

TEST DIRECTION

DIRECTIONS

Read the questions carefully and then choose the ONE best answer to each question.

Be sure to allocate your time carefully so you are able to complete the entire test within the testing session. You may go back and review your answers at any time.

You may use any available space in your test booklet for scratch work.

Questions in this booklet are not actual test questions but they are the samples for commonly asked questions.

This test aims to cover all topics which may appear on the actual test. However some topics may not be covered.

Studying this booklet will be preparing you for the actual test. It will not guarantee improving your test score but it will help you pass your exam on the first attempt.

Some useful tips for answering multiple choice questions;

- Start with the questions that you can easily answer.

- Underline the keywords in the question.

- Be sure to read all the choices given.

- Watch for keywords such as NOT, always, only, all, never, completely.

- Do not forget to answer every question.

CONTINUE ▶

1

A controlled experiment is a scientific test done under controlled conditions. Only one factor is changed at a time, while all others are kept constant.

Which of the following conclusion is true for a controlled experiment?

A) The conclusion must show that the data support the hypothesis.

B) The conclusion must show that the hypothesis was incorrect.

C) The conclusion must be reached for every experiment.

D) The conclusion must relate the data to the hypothesis.

2

What type of bond is responsible for water tension and the formation of water drops?

A) Covalent bond

B) Ionic bond

C) Nuclear bond

D) Hydrogen bond

3

Why is the periodic table of the elements considered as a useful model in science?

A) Because it is a diagram showing a tabular arrangement of the elements into groups with shared physical and chemical properties.

B) Because it shows the historical record of the elements based on the dates of the discovery of the elements.

C) Because it separates the elements into three groups based on the phase when placed at room temperature.

D) Because it consists of a list of elements based on their percent abundance in the Earth's crust and atmosphere.

Alfred Wegener was the first to propose the theory of continental drift in which he explained that continents had changed position over time. However, many scientists rejected his approach despite having some compelling evidence of his claim.

What was the primary scientific reason causing many geologists to reject Wegener's continental drift proposal?

A) He was considered an amateur who was trained in a different scientific discipline.

B) His hypothesis lacked a convincing mechanism to explain what forces moved the continents.

C) He believed his evidence was strong; hence he did not argue the merits of his ideas.

D) His fieldwork lacked the rigor associated with most sciences of the day.

Which of the following is the element present in the largest amount of rocks and minerals?

A) Carbon

B) Magnesium

C) Silicon

D) Hydrogen

The scientific method is a process for experimentation that is used to explore observations and answer questions.

Which of the following is the correct order of the steps in the scientific method?

A) Asking a question, making a hypothesis, testing the hypothesis, drawing conclusions and analyzing results.

B) Asking questions, making a hypothesis, testing the hypothesis, analyzing the results and drawing conclusions.

C) Making a hypothesis, testing the hypothesis, analyzing the results, asking a question and drawing conclusions.

D) Asking a question, analyzing results, making a hypothesis, testing the hypothesis and drawing conclusions.

The Earth atmosphere is composed of many gases that are vital for the survival of all living organisms.

Which of the following pairs of gases lists the two most abundant gases in the Earth's atmosphere?

A) Carbon dioxide and oxygen

B) Carbon dioxide and nitrogen

C) Nitrogen and oxygen

D) Nitrogen and hydrogen

In astronomy, the most commonly used measures of distance are the light year, parsec and astronomical unit.

Which of the following is not a correct explanation?

A) A light-year is a distance that light can travel in one year in a vacuum (space).

B) One parsec is defined as the distance to a star that shifts by one arcsecond from one side of Earth's orbit to the other.

C) The astronomical unit (AU) is a unit of length, roughly the average distance from Earth to the Sun. Astronomical units are usually used to measure distances within our solar system.

D) Light years are usually used to measure distances within our solar system; Astronomical units are used to measure distances between the galaxies.

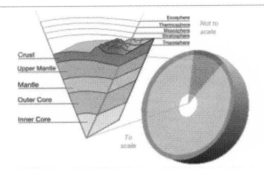

Which of the following can identify the structure of the Earth's core, mantle, and lower crust best?

A) Measuring the intensity and fluctuations of Earth's magnetic field

B) Examining the properties of lava

C) Collecting samples from deep boreholes drilled into Earth

D) Studying the speeds and travel paths of seismic waves passing through Earth

10

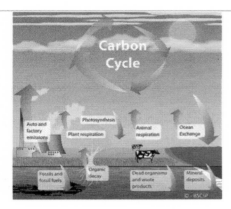

The carbon cycle occurs in the atmosphere, the hydrosphere, the biosphere, and the lithosphere.

Which of the following events describes one step in the movement of carbon from the atmosphere to the lithosphere?

A) Carbonic acid is produced from limestone during weathering.

B) Bicarbonate ions are extracted from seawater during coral reef formation.

C) Carbon dioxide is formed during the decay of biomass.

D) Atomic carbon is absorbed in seawater by deep-ocean sediments.

11

Which of the following scientific skills do you use when you see that the sky is cloudy?

A) Making observation

B) Drawing conclusion

C) Making inference

D) Posing a question

12

A fundamental concept of the cell theory is best summarized by which of the following statements?

A) Each cell has its own DNA and RNA.

B) Living organisms are composed of one or more cells.

C) To maintain health, living organisms rely on specialized cells.

D) Cells break down of molecules to produce energy.

13

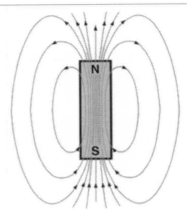

A bar magnet was placed at the bottom of a paper. The iron filings that were previously scattered onto the paper, became aligned along the magnetic field lines similar to that of the image above.

Which of the following causes this behavior of iron filings?

A) The magnetic field of the earth attracts the fillings

B) The fillings are magnetized by the magnetic field

C) The filings are repelled by the induced electric field

D) The magnetic field ionizes the fillings

14

Which of the following about the vapor pressure of the liquid is true when a liquid is at its boiling point?

A) It is greater than the external pressure on the liquid.

B) It is equal to the external pressure on the liquid.

C) It is less than the external pressure on the liquid.

D) It can be either less or greater than the external pressure on the liquid.

15

A scientific team collects data on twenty lakes in different regions of the US to study acid rain. A rain gauge is placed at each lake, and the amount and pH of precipitation that falls each week is recorded. At the same time, the scientists measure the pH of each lake's water and the slope of the ground within 100 meters of each lake's shore.

What is the dependent variable of this study?

A) The measured slope of the ground around each lake

B) The precipitation pH level

C) The amount of precipitation

D) The pH level of each lake's water

16

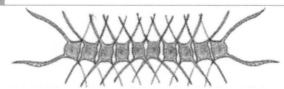

Phytoplanktons are single-celled organisms which are similar to terrestrial plants in that they contain chlorophyll and require sunlight in order to live and grow.

How does a phytoplankton help in balancing the Earth's climate?

A) It takes in ozone and produces diatomic oxygen.

B) It absorbs carbon dioxide and produces oxygen.

C) It uses nitrogen oxides and produces methane.

D) It takes in water vapor and produces carbon dioxide.

17

Which of the following about the vapor pressure of the liquid is true when a liquid is at its boiling point?

A) It is greater than the external pressure on the liquid.

B) It is equal to the external pressure on the liquid.

C) It is less than the external pressure on the liquid.

D) It can be either less or greater than the external pressure on the liquid.

CONTINUE ▶

18

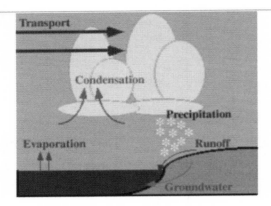

In the hydrologic cycle, water molecules absorb energy during which of the following process?

A) During the formation of ice from water
B) In the formation of a cloud from water vapor
C) The runoff along the land surface
D) The evaporation above the surface of the ocean

19

Which of the following elements in the hemoglobin (a protein found in red blood cells) is responsible for binding oxygen?

A) Calcium
B) Iron
C) Magnesium
D) Titanium

20

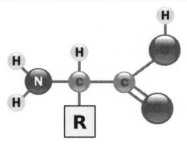

Four major elements make up the majority of most biomolecules. These are carbon, oxygen, nitrogen, and hydrogen. However, carbon is commonly considered as the primary element of life.

Which of the following is the most appropriate explanation for the leading role of carbon in the composition of biomolecules?

A) The six protons in carbon make it easy for it to have an octet through reaction with the alkaline Earth metals.

B) Carbon has the highest electronegativity among the four elements.

C) Carbon is in its solid phase when place at room temperature.

D) Carbon has four valence electrons which allow it to form bonds with other atoms in various ways.

21

Onshore and offshore winds occur over the areas where land masses meet large bodies of water.

Which of the following is the reason why onshore and offshore winds occur?

A) Water has a higher specific heat than land

B) The land has a higher specific heat than water

C) The land absorbs more thermal energy

D) Water cannot absorb as much thermal energy as the land

22

An **ideal gas** is a theoretical gas composed of many randomly moving point particles whose only interactions are perfectly elastic collisions.

For an ideal gas when all other conditions are constant which of the following variables are inversely proportional?

A) Pressure and temperature

B) Pressure and the number of moles

C) Pressure and volume

D) No two variables are inversely proportional

23

John wants to investigate the relationship between the effort needed to slide a given object along an inclined plane and the slope of the inclined plane.

What type of inclined planes should John use?

A) Those inclined planes that are made up of the same materials and the same length, but having different slopes.

B) Those inclined planes that have different lengths, but are made of the same material and having the same slope.

C) Those inclined planes of the same length, but having different slopes and made of different materials.

D) Those inclined planes that are made up of different materials but have the same slope and length.

24

Eutrophication is the process by which a body of water becomes enriched in dissolved nutrients (such as phosphates) that stimulate the growth of aquatic plant life usually resulting in the depletion of dissolved oxygen.

How is it possible to conclude that eutrophication of bodies of water has occurred?

A) By testing for the level of water acidity

B) By having greater species diversity in the water massive algae blooms

C) By having a vibrant, productive aquatic ecosystem

D) By having massive algae blooms

25

Due to which of the following an enormous amount of energy is released in an atomic explosion?

A) The result of the conversion of chemical energy into nuclear energy

B) The result of the conversions of neutrons into protons

C) The result of the conversion of mechanical energy into nuclear energy

D) The result of the conversion of mass into energy

26

Evolution is a theory about the origin of life. It is the process by which organisms change over time as a result of changes in heritable physical or behavioral traits.

Which of the following does not support the evolution?

A) Analogous structures

B) Comparative anatomy

C) Organic chemistry

D) Comparison of DNA among organisms

27

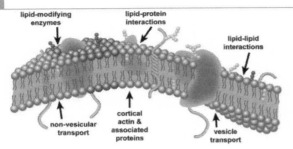

The cell membrane is a very thin membrane, composed of lipids and protein that surrounds the cytoplasm of a cell and controls the passage of substances into and out of the cell.

Which of the following is not true about the cell membrane?

A) It is made from phospholipids.

B) It controls the matter transport within the cell.

C) The cell membrane is the same as the cell wall in plants.

D) Both animal and plant cells have a cell membrane.

28

A galaxy is a gravitationally bound system of stars, stellar remnants, interstellar gasses, dust, and dark matter. Recent estimates made by astronomers say that there are more than a billion galaxies in the observable universe and they are usually categorized based on their shape.

Which of the following shape is taken by our galaxy, the Milky Way?

A) Spiral Galaxy

B) Cloud Galaxy

C) Elliptical Galaxy

D) Irregular Galaxy

29

Whenever a baker is cooking, he always set his oven 50 degrees higher than the suggested temperature of the recipe because the oven's thermometer is consistently 50 degrees off.

Which of the following best describes the reliability of the baker's oven?

A) The baker's oven is not reliable and not correct.

B) The baker's oven is reliable but not correct.

C) The baker's oven is reliable and correct.

D) The baker's oven is not reliable but correct.

30

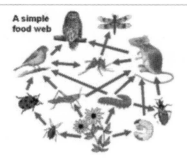

A food web is a natural interconnection of food chains and a graphical representation of what-eats-what in an ecological community.

In a food web, which of the following do the consumers do?

A) Form the base of the trophic pyramid

B) Make their food

C) Exhibit a heterotrophic mode of nutrition

D) Get energy directly from the Sun

31

Anabolism, constructive metabolism, is the synthesis of complex molecules in living organisms from simpler ones together with the storage of energy.

Which of the following is an example of anabolism?

A) The disintegration of proteins into amino acids

B) Disintegration of large molecules into smaller molecules

C) Forming of small molecules from large molecules

D) Forming of proteins from amino acids

32

There is a relationship between the Celsius and Fahrenheit scales for temperature. It is formulated by $F=1.8C+32$. At what temperature both scales show the same value?

A) -40

B) 24

C) 32

D) 180

33

Which of the following about the mass number is correct?

A) It is the sum of the number of protons and neutrons present in the nucleus

B) It is always less than its atomic number

C) It is more than the atomic weight

D) It is same as the atomic number

34

Biological diversity means the variability among living organisms from all sources including, inter alia, terrestrial, marine and other aquatic ecosystems. Diversity can be within species, between species, and of ecosystems.

Which of the following is not true of diversity?

A) Skeletons are being similar to allow for diversity

B) There would be extinction if no diversity

C) There would be extinction if no diversity

D) Fossil evidence supports diversity

35

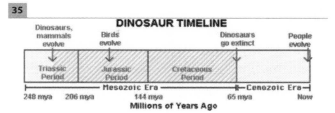

Scientists believe the rapid evolution and diversification of species that occurred at the beginning of the Mesozoic era was the consequence of which of the following?

A) The breakup of the supercontinent Pangaea in the Late Paleozoic period

B) Changes in atmospheric composition resulting from the appearance of photosynthetic organisms

C) The extinction of the majority of species near the end of the Permian period

D) Changes in the rate of genetic mutations resulting from the Sun's increased output of harmful radiation

36

For a researcher, which of the following describes the purpose of identifying first the variables of a particular study?

A) Because variables are the factors that can change and are supposed to be the main focus of the research

B) Because researchers always aim to influence a variable in their particular study

C) Because a variable must be expressed numerically prior to the beginning of any research study

D) Because variables are the control elements that are supposed to remain unchanged throughout the entire study

37

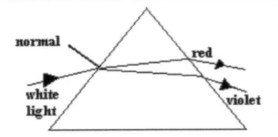

Which of the following phenomena is exhibited above when the white light passes through the prism?

A) Dispersion

B) Superposition

C) Diffusion

D) Reflection

38

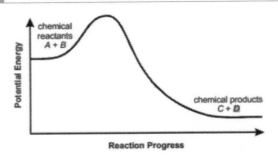

What is the indication of the higher potential energy of the reactants compared to the products?

A) As the products form, chemical energy will increase.

B) As the reactants combine, kinetic energy will decrease.

C) During the reaction, heat energy will be released.

D) During the reaction, heat energy will be absorbed.

39

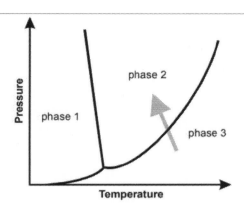

In the water phase-change above, which of the following processes is represented by the gray arrow?

A) Evaporation or the change from liquid to gas

B) Melting or the change from solid to liquid

C) Freezing or the change from liquid to solid

D) Condensation or the change from gas to liquid

40

Greenhouse Gases in the atmosphere absorbs and emits radiation within the thermal infrared range. Some of the Greenhouse Gases are water vapor, carbon dioxide, nitrous oxide, etc.

Which of the following is also a greenhouse gas?

A) Propane

B) Methane

C) Helium

D) Butane

41

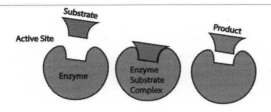

Enzymes are biological catalysts which speed up chemical reactions.

Which of the following is not true of enzymes?

A) They are made of proteins.
B) At high temperatures, they are deformed.
C) They work at a wide range of pH.
D) The enzyme is the lock and substrate is the key.

42

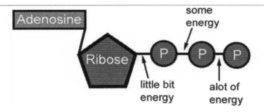

ATP (Adenosine triphosphate) is the principal molecule for storing and transferring energy in cells.

In which of the following stages ATP is generated most?

A) Chemiosmosis
B) Glycolysis
C) Fermentation
D) The Krebs cycle

43

Natural selection is one of the basic mechanisms of evolution. Darwin's theory of natural selection states that organisms which are better adapted to their environment tend to survive and produce more offspring.

Which of the following is true about natural selection?

A) It acts on the genotype
B) It does not happen instantly
C) It is a phenomenon of plants only
D) It acts on the phenotype

The highest level of organization for living things is the biosphere which encompasses all other levels.

The biological levels of organization of living things are arranged from the simplest to the most complex.

Cell: (1)   Tissue: (4)

Organelle: (2)   Organ: (5)

Organ System: (3)   Organism: (6)

Which of the following identifies the correct sequence of the organization of living things?

A) (1) – (2) – (4) – (5) – (3) – (6)
B) (2) – (1) – (4) – (5) – (3) – (6)
C) (2) – (1) – (5) – (4) – (3) – (6)
D) (2) – (1) – (4) – (5) – (6) – (3)

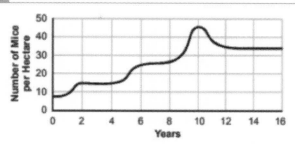

Based on the graph above that illustrates change over time in a population of nonnative mice in a forest, what is the approximate number of the ecosystem's carrying capacity for the mouse population?

A) 15 mice per hectare.
B) 25 mice per hectare.
C) 35 mice per hectare.
D) 45 mice per hectare.

46

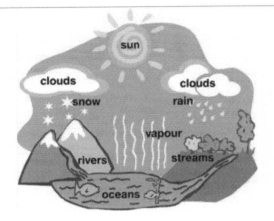

The water cycle is the cycle of processes by which water circulates between the earth's oceans, atmosphere, and land, involving precipitation as rain and snow, drainage in streams and rivers, and return to the atmosphere by evaporation and transpiration.

What is true of the water cycle?

A) Some part of the water is groundwater.
B) Two percent of the water is fixed and unavailable.
C) The ocean currents drive the water cycle.
D) Surface water is unavailable if iced.

47

Abiotic factor is a nonliving condition or thing, as climate or habitat, which influences or affects an ecosystem and the organisms in it. Abiotic factors can determine which species of organisms will survive in a given environment.

Which of the following is not an abiotic factor?

A) Rainfall
B) Soil quality
C) Temperature
D) Bacteria

48

A group of researchers is conducting a study about the behavior of animals that thrive in the hottest deserts of Africa to understand what these creatures need to survive in such a harsh climate. They are measuring how much they eat and drink per day as well as analyzing their activity during extremely hot temperatures.

As a generalization, which of the following is an application of the results of their study?

A) The results can only be applied to the environment where the researcher studied personally.

B) The results can be applied to similar environments, such as a desert climate in South America.

C) The results can be applied to the behavior of all animals, regardless of the climate they live in.

D) The results can't be applied to another area since generalization can only be used in qualitative studies.

49

Acid rain is caused by emissions of sulfur dioxide and nitrogen oxide, which react with the water molecules in the atmosphere to produce acids.

Which of the following about the acid rains is not correct?

A) When sulfurous gases such as sulfur dioxide (SO2) react with water they produce ammonia.

B) Scientific evidence has linked acid rain to decreased fish and wildlife populations, degraded lakes and streams, and human health hazards.

C) Acid rain became a household term in the 1980s when unchecked emissions from industry and motor vehicles were blamed for causing environmental deterioration.

D) Acid rain is a result of air pollution because sulfur dioxide and nitrogen oxides are bi-products from burning fuels in electric utilities and from other industrial and natural sources.

50

Bacteria can multiply very quickly. Mycobacteria has a doubling time of around 15 minutes. If 100 bacteria are left alone, how many bacteria will be after 2 hours?

A) 12,400
B) 18,400
C) 25,600
D) 36,600

51

A Doctor wants to study the effectiveness of a CPAP Machines for sleep apnea. The Doctor records data on three groups of test subjects. The first group includes people who suffer from Apnea and are given the CPAP Machine. The second group includes people who suffer from apnea and are not given the CPAP Machine. The third group includes people who do not suffer from apnea and are given the experimental CPAP Machine.

Which of the following describes the research design for this study?

A) Observational study
B) Controlled experiment
C) Sample survey
D) None of the above

52

• A dead tree decays.

• The top of a hill erodes slowly.

• A star uses up its nuclear fuel over years.

• A bottle of cologne is opened and the molecules spread throughout the room.

Which of the following scientific principles is illustrated in the four phenomena described above?

A) Physical balance called equilibrium
B) A reaction to something of a response
C) A state of disorder or entropy
D) A state of total confusion with no order called chaos

53

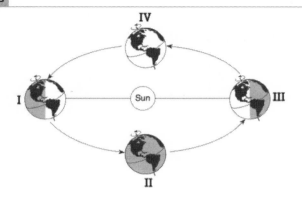

The figure above shows Earth orbiting the Sun while it is rotating about its axis once every 24 hours.

Which change in seasons occurs in the Northern Hemisphere at position IV?

A) Winter is ending, and spring is beginning.

B) Spring is ending, and summer is beginning.

C) Summer is ending, and fall is beginning.

D) Fall is ending, and winter is beginning.

54

Reactants	Observation
P and Q	Turns red after three hours
Q and R	No change
P and R	No change
P, Q and R	Turns red after two minutes

The reactants P, Q, and R given above are colorless liquids.

Which of the following explanation is correct?

A) In the reaction of P and Q, R acts as a catalyst.

B) The combined product of Q and R reacts with P.

C) The combined product of P and Q reacts with R.

D) In the reaction between Q and R, P acts as a catalyst.

CONTINUE ▶

What must scientists do to isolate the relationship between two variables in an experiment?

A) Experiment with a laboratory setting

B) Predict the full range of possible outcomes of the experiment

C) Control the conditions under which the experiment is carried out

D) Limit the scope of the experiment to the investigation of known facts

The intrusive igneous rocks that are composed of unusually large crystals are called pegmatites.

Which condition can typically result in the formation of pegmatites?

A) The solidification of magma bodies below the extinct volcanoes

B) The crystallization of rocks at slow rates and the high temperatures near the boundary between the mantle and the crust

C) The solidification of the granitic batholiths, leaving fluid-rich residual melt

D) The crystallization at relatively fast rates as magma flows rapidly away from its source to form a sill

57

Environmental toxins can accumulate to high levels in organisms at the top of the food chain. If DDT is present in an ecosystem, in which of the following organisms will the DDT concentration be highest?

A) Frog

B) Eagle

C) Grasshopper

D) Crabgrass

58

Which of the following is used to test the effect of scent on a person's mood by exposing them to a scent and observing their reactions?

A) Laboratory Observation

B) Naturalistic Observation

C) Experiment Observation

D) Two-Way Mirror Observation

59

Which of the following is not true about decomposers?

A) Phosphorous is added back to the soil by decomposers.

B) Ammonification is the formation of ammonia or its compounds by decomposition of organic matter.

C) The Carbon accumulated in durable organic material is recycled by decomposers.

D) Decomposers belong to the Genus Escherichia.

60

Which of the following information is provided by the hypothesis during a scientific investigation?

A) A question that can be answered by researching existing literature

B) A format for outlining the approach to be used in the investigation

C) A summary of previous research on the topic being investigated

D) A proposed explanation for the phenomena being investigated

SECTION 4 - LIFE SCIENCE & SCIENTIFIC REASONING

#	Answer	Topic	Subtopic	#	Answer	Topic	Subtopic	#	Answer	Topic	Subtopic	#	Answer	Topic	Subtopic
1	D	TB	S2	16	B	TB	S2	31	C	TB	S2	46	B	TB	S2
2	D	TB	S2	17	B	TB	S2	32	A	TB	S2	47	D	TB	S2
3	A	TB	S2	18	D	TB	S2	33	A	TB	S2	48	B	TB	S2
4	B	TB	S2	19	B	TB	S2	34	A	TB	S2	49	A	TB	S2
5	A	TB	S2	20	D	TB	S2	35	C	TB	S2	50	C	TB	S2
6	B	TB	S2	21	A	TB	S2	36	A	TB	S2	51	B	TB	S2
7	C	TB	S2	22	C	TB	S2	37	A	TB	S2	52	C	TB	S2
8	C	TB	S2	23	A	TB	S2	38	C	TB	S2	53	D	TB	S2
9	D	TB	S2	24	D	TB	S2	39	D	TB	S2	54	A	TB	S2
10	B	TB	S2	25	D	TB	S2	40	B	TB	S2	55	C	TB	S2
11	A	TB	S2	26	C	TB	S2	41	C	TB	S2	56	C	TB	S2
12	B	TB	S2	27	C	TB	S2	42	A	TB	S2	57	B	TB	S2
13	B	TB	S2	28	A	TB	S2	43	D	TB	S2	58	A	TB	S2
14	B	TB	S2	29	B	TB	S2	44	B	TB	S2	59	D	TB	S2
15	D	TB	S2	30	C	TB	S2	45	C	TB	S2	60	D	TB	S2

Topics & Subtopics

Code	Description	Code	Description
SB2	Basic Science	TB	Science

TEST DIRECTION

DIRECTIONS

Read the questions carefully and then choose the ONE best answer to each question.

Be sure to allocate your time carefully so you are able to complete the entire test within the testing session. You may go back and review your answers at any time.

You may use any available space in your test booklet for scratch work.

Questions in this booklet are not actual test questions but they are the samples for commonly asked questions.

This test aims to cover all topics which may appear on the actual test. However some topics may not be covered.

Studying this booklet will be preparing you for the actual test. It will not guarantee improving your test score but it will help you pass your exam on the first attempt.

Some useful tips for answering multiple choice questions;

- Start with the questions that you can easily answer.

- Underline the keywords in the question.

- Be sure to read all the choices given.

- Watch for keywords such as NOT, always, only, all, never, completely.

- Do not forget to answer every question.

112   CONTINUE ▶

1

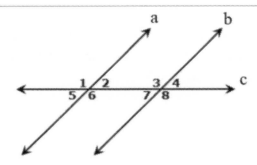

The drawing shows parallel lines *a* and *b* intersected by transversal *c*. Which of the following statements about the angles is not correct?

A) 1 and 6 are opposite angles.

B) 4 and 8 are complementary angles.

C) 3 and 4 are supplementary angles.

D) 2 and 7 are alternate interior angles.

2

Two triangles are similar. The sides of the first triangle are 5, 9, and 12. The biggest side of the second triangle is 36. Find the perimeter of the second triangle?

A) 26

B) 42

C) 64

D) 78

3

If the volume of a cube is equal to the total surface area of that cube, then what is the length of one side of the cube?

A) 6

B) 36

C) 108

D) 216

4

If the radius of a circle is doubled, then the area of the new circle is;

A) One-fourth of the area of the original circle.

B) One-half of the area of the original circle.

C) If the radius of a circle is doubled, then the area of the new circle is;

D) Four times the area of the original circle.

5

Which of the following Fahrenheit values is equivalent to -10°C?

A) 22°F

B) 32°F

C) 14°F

D) 18°F

CONTINUE ▶

6

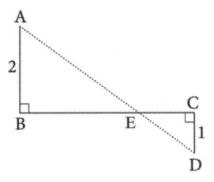

In the figure above what is the length of EC, if BC=24?

A) 6

B) 8

C) 12

D) 18

7

How does the volume of a cylinder change if the radius of its base is doubled and its height is halved?

A) The volume does not change.

B) The volume is halved.

C) The volume is doubled.

D) The volume is quadrupled.

8

The circumference of the circular table on Andrew's porch is 48π inches. What is the radius of the table?

A) 18 inches

B) 24 inches

C) 48 inches

D) 96 inches

9

If the volume of a cube is equal to the total surface area of that cube, then what is the length of one side of the cube?

A) 6

B) 36

C) 108

D) 216

10

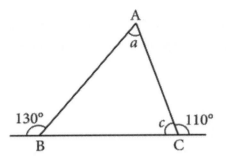

What is the sum of the angles $a + c$?

A) 50

B) 60

C) 70

D) 130

11

At a particular time of the day, the shadow of a 6' tree is 8' long. The shadow of a building at this same time is 48' long. How tall is the building?

A) 14

B) 24

C) 36

D) 64

12

How many right angles are formed by the edges of a cube?

A) 16

B) 20

C) 24

D) 30

13

The interior dimensions of a rectangular oil tank are 7 feet long, 6 feet wide, and 5 feet high. The oil level in the tank is 4 feet tall. If all of the oil in this tank is poured into an empty second tank that has interior dimensions 8 feet long, 4 feet wide, and 9 feet high, what is the height in feet of the oil in the second tank?

A) 2.75

B) 3.75

C) 5.25

D) 10.5

14

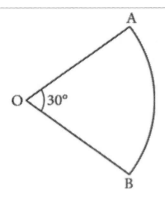

The figure above is 30° segment of the circle whose center is O. If the arc length of AB is 6π, then what is the radius OB of the circle?

A) 6

B) 12

C) 36

D) 72

15

	Length	Height	Width
A	4cm	8cm	3cm
B	6cm	12cm	4cm

Measures of objects A and B are given in the table above. If both objects are made from the same material what would be the weight of the object B in terms of the object A?

A) Two times lighter

B) The same weight

C) Three times heavier

D) Four times heavier

16

If 1 furlong = 40 rods and 1 rod = .25 chains, then 3.5 furlongs is equal to how many chains?

A) 7.5

B) 10

C) 35

D) 21

17

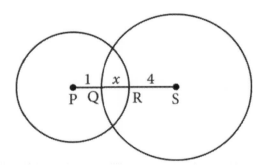

P and S are the centers of the circles. PQ=1, RS=4, and QR=x. What is x if the radius of the circle with the center S is two times the radius of the circle with the center P?

A) 1

B) 2

C) 3

D) 4

18

Chad is painting the outside of a box that is in the shape of a rectangular prism. Its length is 18 centimeters, its width is 6 centimeters, and its height is 3 centimeters.

What is the surface area of the box in square centimeters?

A) 300

B) 360

C) 480

D) 180

19

A cylindrically shaped beaker whose base radius is 8 cm is filled with water to a height of 9cm above the base. A metal sphere with a diameter of 6cm is submerged in the water.

How high above the base of the beaker is the new water level, in cm?

A) 11

B) 11.25

C) 11.5

D) 12

20

Eddie runs four laps around 600m track at a constant speed. If it takes Eddie 20 minutes to run all four laps, what is his speed in meters per second?

A) 1

B) 2

C) 3

D) 4

21

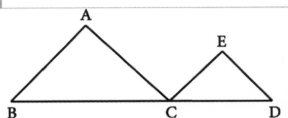

ABC and ECD are equilateral triangles. B, C, and D are collinear and BD = 15. What is the sum of the perimeters of the triangles?

A) 15

B) 27

C) 30

D) 45

22

Andreas has a piece of rectangular paper that is 24 inches wide by 32 inches long. He drew a straight line along the diagonal of the paper. What is the length of the line Andreas drew?

A) 40 inches

B) 56 inches

C) 6.32 inches

D) 7.48 inches

23

If the school is 12 miles away from Anne's house and Starbucks is 4 miles away from the school, which of the following conclusions must be true?

A) Starbucks is exactly 8 miles from Anne's house.

B) Anne's house is closer to the school than Starbucks.

C) Anne's house is east of the school.

D) Anne's house is at most 16 miles from Starbucks.

24

Faye is painting the outside of a box that is in the shape of a rectangular prism. Its length is 18 centimeters, its width is 6 centimeters, and its height is 3 centimeters.

What is the surface area of the box in square centimeters?

A) 180

B) 300

C) 360

D) 480

25

ABC is an isoscales triangle. $AB = 3x - 2$, $BC = 2x + 4$, and $AC = x + 5$. If $AB = BC$, then what is the perimeter of this triangle?

A) 16

B) 25

C) 37

D) 43

26

A manufacturing company puts 24 cans into each box they send to a store. Each can has a diameter of 3 inches and a height of 9 inches.

What is the approximate total volume, in cubic inches, of the cans in each box the company sends to a store? (Use 3.14 for π)

A) 6,104.16 cubic inches

B) 1,526.04 cubic inches

C) 63.585 cubic inches

D) 42.36 cubic inches

CONTINUE ▶

27

If 1 pound = 16 ounces then how many ounces are equal to 26 pounds?

A) 416

B) 351

C) 716

D) 530

28

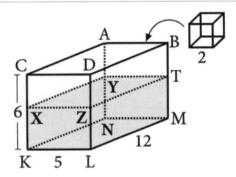

In the water tank of a rectangular prism given above, width, length, and height are 5cm, 12 cm and 6 cm. XYZT shows the water level in the tank. If MT=2BT, at most how many cubes of size 2cm can be placed into the tank such that there will be no overflow?

A) 8

B) 15

C) 30

D) 45

29

If each side of a cube is increased by 10%, how does the volume of the cube change?

A) The volume also increases by 10%

B) The volume also increases by 21%

C) The volume also increases by 30%

D) The volume also increases by 33.1%

30

A seriously injured inmate will be taken to a medical center by a correction officer. The distance to the medical center is 72 miles. If the transport vehicle moves at a constant speed of 48 mph, how many minutes will it take to go to the medical center?

A) 40

B) 90

C) 150

D) 5400

31

The water tank of a fire truck is 4-meter length, 3 meters wide and 2 meters high. If water is pumped at speed if 2-meter cube per minute, how many minutes will it take to finish the water in the tank?

A) 96

B) 48

C) 24

D) 12

32

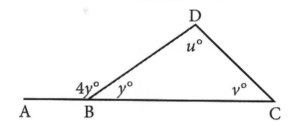

Given the figure above, if $u-v=26$, then what is the value of v?

A) 26

B) 36

C) 59

D) 85

SECTION 5 - MATH - GEOMETRY & MEASUREMENT

#	Answer	Topic	Subtopic	#	Answer	Topic	Subtopic	#	Answer	Topic	Subtopic	#	Answer	Topic	Subtopic
1	C	TB	S2	9	A	TB	S2	17	B	TB	S2	25	D	TB	S2
2	D	TB	S2	10	B	TB	S2	18	B	TB	S2	26	B	TB	S2
3	A	TB	S2	11	C	TB	S2	19	B	TB	S2	27	A	TB	S2
4	D	TB	S2	12	C	TB	S2	20	B	TB	S2	28	B	TB	S2
5	C	TB	S2	13	C	TB	S2	21	D	TB	S2	29	D	TB	S2
6	B	TB	S2	14	C	TB	S2	22	A	TB	S2	30	B	TB	S2
7	C	TB	S2	15	C	TB	S2	23	D	TB	S2	31	A	TB	S2
8	B	TB	S2	16	C	TB	S2	24	C	TB	S2	32	C	TB	S2

Topics & Subtopics

Code	Description	Code	Description
SB2	Geometry and Measurement	TB	Mathematics

TEST DIRECTION

Read the questions carefully and then choose the ONE best answer to each question.

Be sure to allocate your time carefully so you are able to complete the entire test within the testing session. You may go back and review your answers at any time.

You may use any available space in your test booklet for scratch work.

Questions in this booklet are not actual test questions but they are the samples for commonly asked questions.

This test aims to cover all topics which may appear on the actual test. However some topics may not be covered.

Studying this booklet will be preparing you for the actual test. It will not guarantee improving your test score but it will help you pass your exam on the first attempt.

Some useful tips for answering multiple choice questions;

- Start with the questions that you can easily answer.

- Underline the keywords in the question.

- Be sure to read all the choices given.

- Watch for keywords such as NOT, always, only, all, never, completely.

- Do not forget to answer every question.

1

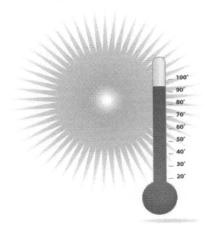

Heat is defined as the quality of being hot.

Which root word means "heat"?

A) therm
B) theo
C) leg
D) hydr

2

Most people believe happiness is a matter of inborn temperament.

Which one indicates best if there is an English grammar problem with the sentence given above?

A) "people" should be "peoples"
B) "happiness" should be "happyness"
C) "is" should be "are"
D) There are no grammar problems

3

A **prefix** is defined as a letter or group of letters that is added at the beginning of a word in order to change its meaning.

Which prefix means "opposite"?

A) re-
B) dis-
C) semi-
D) pre-

4

Which of the following sentences does not contain a modifier error?

A) I thought that his flute sounded terrible.
B) The price doesn't make any difference to Edward.
C) Rosemary should clean her room more thorough.
D) It was the delightfullest trip I have ever taken.

5

Which of the following word is misspelled?

A) Feirce
B) Exercise
C) Stabilize
D) Proceed

6

Which of the following phrases obeys the rules of capitalization?

A) prepared a bbq party
B) the Morris sisters
C) attorney andrew smith
D) in their House Last thanksgiving

7

Which of the following stages is not part of the writing process?

A) Making an outline
B) Starting with an introductory paragraph
C) Writing a thesis sentence for each body paragraph
D) Ending with a thesis sentence

8

Which of the following sentences below is punctuated correctly?

A) The colorful bird flew across the river; freely enjoying the summer season.
B) The colorful bird flew across the river: freely enjoying the summer season.
C) The colorful bird flew across the river, freely enjoying, the summer season.
D) The colorful bird flew across the river, freely enjoying the summer season.

9

A **suffix** is a letter or group of letters that is added to the end of a word to change its meaning.

Which suffix means "more"?

A) -ful
B) -er
C) -ion
D) -est

10

"Philip likes ornate artwork, extravagant clothes, and immoderate cars. He is so frugal that he hangs cheap posters on his walls and drives an economy hatchback car."

Which of the following word best suits to the examples of 'Cheap posters' and 'economy hatchback car' in the paragraph given above?

A) Extravagant
B) Unbalanced
C) None of these
D) Frugal

11

A relative pronoun is a word that joins two parts of a sentence together to make one sentence.

Which of the following does not contain correct relative pronoun?

A) The dog that bit the boy was tied up.
B) I spoke to a man whose name was Arvin.
C) This is the man to who the cat belongs.
D) The briefcase which contained the jewelry was stolen.

12

Which of the following sentences does not have any error in subject verb agreement?

A) Each of those tshirts cost too much.
B) There are a greater possibility of seeing the lion.
C) The students in the geometry class have finished taking the exam.
D) Nobody in our class want to be the moderator of the meeting.

13

Unlike the … skin of a frog, that of a toad is much more textured and … .

From the options below pick the most suitable words to accurately complete the sentence given above.

A) green; brown
B) tough; scaly
C) slick; slimy
D) smooth; bumpy

14

Which of the following sentences does not have any error in subject verb agreement?

A) Does either of the boys own a bicycle?
B) Every one of these busses carry forty passengers.
C) My neighbor and closest friend are Anthony Dabon.
D) Kristina, along with the rest of the girls, have already gone to the cafeteria.

15

Punctuation marks are used to create sense, clarity, and stress in sentences.

Which of the following phrases below has the correct punctuation?

A) "Why don't you like her?" his friend asked.

B) "Why don"t you like her" his friend asked.

C) "Why don't you like her," his friend asked.

D) "Why dont you like her?" his friend asked.

16

A **modifier** is a word, phrase, or clause which functions as an adjective or an adverb to describe a word or make its meaning more specific.

Which of the following sentences does not contain a modifier error?

A) The story begins very interestingly.

B) They were talking loud.

C) Do you consider math or algebra hardest?

D) Mt. Kota Kinabalu is the higher mountain in Java.

17

What is the proper alphabetical order of the following names?

1. Maxwell, Alexander

2. Maxwell, Alexandra

3. Maxwell, Alexandro

4. Maxwell, Alexandre

A) 1, 2, 3, 4

B) 2, 3, 1, 4

C) 1, 4, 2, 3

D) 1, 2, 4, 3

18

The teacher asks students to include drafts as well as final versions of the writing samples in their portfolio.

Which of the following is the main benefit of using this type of portfolio with students?

A) It documents students' learning abilities over time.

B) It interprets one student's performance in relation to other students.

C) It provides a reliable means of predicting students' future performances.

D) It enables the teacher to determine students' mastery of large domains of content.

19

Which of the following sentences does not contain a modifier error?

A) Brush your teeth well after eating something.

B) Have you ever seen anyone drive graceful?

C) The new rules are more stricter than the old ones.

D) Kevin's plan sounded foolishly tohis friends.

20

Tense expresses the time at which the action described by the verb takes place. The major tenses are past, present, and future.

Sentences and the tenses of them are given below. Which of the following sentences does not contain correct verb tense?

A) Present Tense; "What are the stores like around here?"

B) Past Tense; " Was there anybody in when you opened the door?"

C) Future Tense; "Will Sam be able to mend that broken door?"

D) Present Tense; "What will you do when this course finishes?"

21

A third-grade teacher is planning a persuasive writing unit as classroom activity. Although the students have done persuasive writing in the past, they did not focus on visual persuasion.

Which of the following visual literacy skills should the teacher highlight during the activity?

A) Analyzing visuals

B) Comparing visual persuasive pieces

C) Classifying the type of visual emotion and response

D) Recognizing visual cues

22

At which stage of the writing process are free writing, idea mapping, brainstorming, and clustering considered to be the most important?

A) Prewriting

B) Drafting

C) Revising

D) Proofreading

23

Out of the below lines of dialogue, which one has the correct punctuation?

A) "I went to the market" Jane said, "but I didn't find anything I wanted to buy."

B) "I went to the market," Jane said, "but I didn't find anything I wanted to buy."

C) "I went to the market," Jane said "but I didn't find anything I wanted to buy."

D) "I went to the market," Jane said, "But I didn't find anything I wanted to buy."

24

Which tense would you use for describing last year's holiday?

A) Past

B) Present

C) Future

D) Continuous

25

Which of the following sentences has a preposition used in the correct form?

A) She took the bottle down in the shelf.

B) How often do you borrow from the library.

C) You shouldn't look in the sun by binoculars.

D) In order to get to the supermarket I had to drive along your house.

26

Which of the following sentences does not contain a modifier error?

A) Susan prefers a more milder cheese.

B) The new bridge is more safe than the old one.

C) Automobiles run more economically at moderate speeds.

D) The Pistons tried very desperate for a touchdown.

27

A teacher asks a group of English-speaking toddlers to "do something on the piece of paper.

If the toodlers don't know how to read and write, which of following the majority of group will do?

A) Mark the paper
B) Write shape of letters
C) Create scratch that resembles the writing system to which they have been exposed
D) Will do nothing

28

Which of the following sentences does not have any error in subject verb agreement?

A) The infantry constitute the largest division.
B) Under the old boards were a frightened dog.
C) Each of the organizations has a sponsor.
D) Sam, Morgan, and my brother Edward thinks that the Pacers will win.

29

A **modifier** is a word, phrase, or clause which functions as an adjective or an adverb to describe a word or make its meaning more specific.

Which of the following sentences does not contain a modifier error?

A) The story begins very interestingly.
B) They were talking loud.
C) Do you consider math or algebra hardest?
D) Mt. Kota Kinabalu is the higher mountain in Java.

30

Unlike the _____ skin of frogs, toads are much more textured and _____.

From the options below, which of the following has the words that fit the sentence?

A) green; brown
B) tough; scaly
C) slick; slimy
D) smooth; bumpy

CONTINUE ▶

31

Which of the following word is correctly spelled?

A) Magnifisient

B) Asspirations

C) Credential

D) Irrelevent

32

Reading regularly and widely contributes to the development of writing ability.

In which of the following ways can teachers can link reading and writing?

A) Study craft

B) Study genres

C) Study phonics

D) All of the above

33

Which of the following sentences include correct use of demonstrative pronouns?

A) You can eat that apples.

B) That plant needs water.

C) Remember this movie we watched last week.

D) This tests on my table don't have names on them.

34

Which of the following sentences has a preposition used in the correct form?

A) I'm sorry but John's for holiday at the moment.

B) He is of no means certain of what he's doing.

C) Are you looking for anything in particular?

D) The students couldn't get into the steel barricades.

35

Tense expresses the time at which the action described by the verb takes place. The major tenses are past, present, and future.

Sentences and the tenses of them are given below. Which of the following sentences does not contain correct verb tense?

A) Present Tense; "What are the stores like around here?"

B) Past Tense; " Was there anybody in when you opened the door?"

C) Future Tense; "Will Sam be able to mend that broken door?"

D) Present Tense; "What will you do when this course finishes?"

36

A **pronoun** is a word that substitutes for a noun or noun phrase.

Which of the following sentences does not contain a pronoun error?

A) Aielo is coming. Don't let he sees us!

B) Melissa and I are going soon so you can come with us.

C) There is a message for his on the table.

D) Steven watched the children carefully as them crossed the road.

37

Which of the following sentences has a verb used in the correct form?

A) I'll meet Judith in the town tonight.

B) I'll get you something to drink. Coke or tea?

C) What time will your bus leave tomorrow?

D) Luciana can't come. She will take the car to the garage at 5 p.m.

38

Which of the following about the verbs is correct?

A) 'Drove' is the past of 'drive'.

B) 'Felt' is the past of 'fill'.

C) 'Shut' is the past of 'shout'.

D) 'Taught' is the past of 'teach'.

39

Which of the following is not a complete sentence?

A) First, study a lot.
B) Final steps for success.
C) Making an action plan is better.
D) Imagination is more important than knowledge.

40

Which of the following sentences does not have any error in subject verb agreement?

A) Everyone in Mr.Doldi's class were to give a report.
B) Either Aila or Elleny are planning a party.
C) Do either of Kevin or John know how to play baseball?
D) Does Reynaldo or the girls in the Ms.Cohen's class know why radium glows in the dark?

41

Last week John went to the cinema with his brother and a friend. His friend likes horror movies, and his brother likes action movies. They end up watching one of each. They have fun.

In the paragraph given above, in which area some corrections are needed?

A) Referencing pronouns clearly
B) Identifying sentence fragments
C) Creating compound sentences
D) Using the correct verb tense

42

Most people believe happiness is a matter of inborn temperament.

Which of the following indicates the English grammar problem in the sentence above?

A) "people" should be "peoples"
B) "happiness" should be "happyness"
C) "is" should be "are"
D) There are no grammar problems

43

In which of the following sentences is there a redundant word or phrase?

A) She always shows up for work on time.
B) The best parts of her previous proposals are included in the presentation.
C) They are now using GPS technology combined together with GIS mapping.
D) None of the above.

44

Which of the following about the verbs is correct?

A) 'Drove' is the past of 'drive'.
B) 'Felt' is the past of 'fill'.
C) 'Shut' is the past of 'shout'.
D) 'Taught' is the past of 'teach'.

45

Which of the following sentences has a preposition used in the correct form?

A) We must pass this test with all costs.
B) You cannot get a refund for sale goods.
C) We do not have any lilac underwear at stock at the moment.
D) He was shot right between the eyes.

46

Which of the following sentences has a preposition used in the correct form?

A) She took the bottle down in the shelf.
B) How often do you borrow from the library.
C) You shouldn't look in the sun by binoculars.
D) In order to get to the supermarket I had to drive along your house.

47

There is a loophole in the rules concerning academic progress that May allow a student to regain eligibility for financial aid by changing degree programs or by transferring to another college.

Which of the following indicates best if there is an English grammar problem with the sentence given above?

A) "eligibility" should be "elegibility"
B) "programs" should be "programms"
C) "May" should be "may"
D) There are no grammar problems

48

Comparative adjectives compare two nouns like people, places, things, or ideas. On the other hand, **Superlative** adjectives compare more than two nouns.

Which of the following sentences contains correct comparative and/or superlative modifiers with correct spelling and grammar?

A) My computer is more efficient than your.

B) The white coat is warmer then the gray one.

C) My house is the bigger house in the neighborhood.

D) This batch of cookies is the best I've ever made.

49

A **prefix** is an affix which is added to the beginning of a word to modify its meaning.

Which of the following prefixes means "opposite"?

A) re-

B) dis-

C) semi-

D) pre-

50

Capitalization is the act of writing or printing in capital letters or with an initial capital.

Which of the following phrases below follows these rules?

A) Dr. Abby griffin

B) appointed as The

C) new director of current affairs

D) january 2, 2014

51

Which of the following sentences has a preposition used in the correct form?

A) We must pass this test with all costs.

B) You cannot get a refund for sale goods.

C) We do not have any lilac underwear at stock at the moment.

D) He was shot right between the eyes.

52

Which of the following sentences does not have any error in subject verb agreement?

A) Each of those tshirts cost too much.
B) There are a greater possibility of seeing the lion.
C) The students in the geometry class have finished taking the exam.
D) Nobody in our class want to be the moderator of the meeting.

53

You are given the following sentence. Out of the options below, which one indicates best if there is an English grammar problem with it?

There is a loophole in the rules concerning academic progress that May allow a student to regain eligibility for financial aid by changing degree programs or by transferring to another college.

A) "eligibility" should be "elegibility"
B) "programs" should be "programms"
C) "May" should be "may"
D) There are no grammar problems

54

Hydropulping involves grounding the waste with the use of an oxidizing fluid like hypochlorite solution.

Which of the following does the word "grounding" as used in the sentence above most nearly mean?

A) Compressing
B) Descending
C) Confirming
D) Instructing

55

Comparative adjectives compare two nouns like people, places, things, or ideas. On the other hand, **Superlative** adjectives compare more than two nouns.

Which of the following sentences contains correct comparative and/or superlative modifiers with correct spelling and grammar?

A) My computer is more efficient than your.
B) The white coat is warmer then the gray one.
C) My house is the bigger house in the neighborhood.
D) This batch of cookies is the best I've ever made.

56

Which tense would you use for describing last year's holiday?

A) Past
B) Present
C) Future
D) Continuous

57

Which of the following sentences does not contain a modifier error?

A) Susan prefers a more milder cheese.
B) The new bridge is more safe than the old one.
C) Automobiles run more economically at moderate speeds.
D) The Pistons tried very desperate for a touchdown.

58

Which of the following sentences does not have any error in subject verb agreement?

A) Each of us was playing very good.
B) Most of the horses in the race is there for the first time.
C) Every one of my friends have read this book about animals.
D) Either the orchestra or the choir give a free concerts a month.

59

Which of the following sentences does not contain a modifier error?

A) I thought that his flute sounded terrible.
B) The price doesn't make any difference to Edward.
C) Rosemary should clean her room more thorough.
D) It was the delightfullest trip I have ever taken.

60

Which of the following given sentences has the most accurate English grammar usage?

A) The boost in work compensations can only be done after a through examination.

B) The tenants are obliged to follow all the stipulations in the contracts; however, Marina has had an exclusive deal drawn up.

C) The data on innovation in the work environment can be found on our site.

D) As indicated by the contract, all employees must finish the trainings before start to work.

61

Preposition is a function word that typically combines with a noun phrase to describe a relationship between other words in a sentence.

Which of the following sentences has a preposition used in the correct form?

A) His life depends on a heart transplant.

B) The police ran for the thieves but didn't catch them.

C) Could you turn left in the next junction.

D) He is the fastest man on the world.

62

Preposition is a function word that typically combines with a noun phrase to describe a relationship between other words in a sentence.

Which of the following sentences has a preposition used in the correct form?

A) His life depends on a heart transplant.

B) The police ran for the thieves but didn't catch them.

C) Could you turn left in the next junction.

D) He is the fastest man on the world.

63

Which of the following sentences has a preposition used in the correct form?

A) I'm sorry but John's for holiday at the moment.

B) He is of no means certain of what he's doing.

C) Are you looking for anything in particular?

D) The students couldn't get into the steel barricades.

64

Which of the following sentences has any error in subject verb agreement?

A) The length of these trucks is twenty feet.
B) Everyone in the physics course have had to fill out an additional form.
C) The number of immigrants in Turkey is astounding.
D) One of the basketball players is hurt.

65

Which of the following sentences does not have any error in subject verb agreement?

A) Everyone in Mr.Doldi's class were to give a report.
B) Either Aila or Elleny are planning a party.
C) Do either of Kevin or John know how to play baseball?
D) Does Reynaldo or the girls in the Ms.Cohen's class know why radium glows in the dark?

66

Which of the following sentences does not contain a modifier error?

A) Brush your teeth well after eating something.
B) Have you ever seen anyone drive graceful?
C) The new rules are more stricter than the old ones.
D) Kevin's plan sounded foolishly tohis friends.

67

Which of the following sentences does not have any error in subject verb agreement?

A) The infantry constitute the largest division.
B) Under the old boards were a frightened dog.
C) Each of the organizations has a sponsor.
D) Sam, Morgan, and my brother Edward thinks that the Pacers will win.

68

Evaluation essay demonstrates the overall quality or lack of a particular product, business, place, service or program.

Which of the following are the three key elements of the evaluative essay?

A) Evidence, Reasoning, Criteria
B) Judgment, Background, Compare/Contrast
C) Plot, Characters, Storyline
D) Judgment, Criteria, Evidence

69

Punctuation is used to create sense, clarity, and stress in sentences. Which of the below phrases has the correct punctuation?

A) Her moms car
B) Her mom"s car
C) Her mom's car
D) Her mom's car'

70

Which of the following sentences does not have any error in subject verb agreement?

A) Each of us was playing very good.
B) Most of the horses in the race is there for the first time.
C) Every one of my friends have read this book about animals.
D) Either the orchestra or the choir give a free concerts a month.

71

"It is the **biggest** planet in the solar system, **spins** very **rapidly** on **it's** axis."

Which of the following words in the sentence given above has an error in terms of grammar or punctuation?

A) biggest
B) it's
C) rapidly
D) spins

72

Which of the following sentences has a verb used in the correct form?

A) I'll meet Judith in the town tonight.
B) I'll get you something to drink. Coke or tea?
C) What time will your bus leave tomorrow?
D) Luciana can't come. She will take the car to the garage at 5 p.m.

73

Which of the following sentences has any error in subject verb agreement?

A) The length of these trucks is twenty feet.
B) Everyone in the physics course have had to fill out an additional form.
C) The number of immigrants in Turkey is astounding.
D) One of the basketball players is hurt.

74

Text-based instructional strategy involves teaching reading through exposure to many different types of texts.

For which of the following students text-based instruction may not be suitable?

A) Students who read slow
B) Students with special needs
C) Students who don't like to reading
D) Students who find phonics instruction boring

75

Five-year-old Kevin writes the letter K all around the edges of a card, with the picture of a dog image, and says, "This is my doggy. It says Floppy."

Understanding of which of the following is shown above?

A) The function of print
B) The alphabetic knowledge
C) Hand and eye coordination
D) How words are decrypted

Because of Chelsey's ... attitude, many were ... to trust her as leader of the science group.

Which of the following words are the most suitable to accurately complete the sentence given above?

A) apathetic; compelled

B) uncaring; reluctant

C) good; unwilling

D) negative; eager

You are given the following sentence. How many of the words contain letters that seem to appear more than once in that word?

"Going to a party alone can be an awkward social experience, but only if you let it become one."

A) 4

B) 5

C) 6

D) None of the above

Students are in various levels of the writing process and they are working on self-selected topics. Teachers are meeting with individual or small groups of students to confer and help move them along with their writing.

Which of the following teaching models is explained above?

A) Writing workshop

B) Direct instruction

C) Literature circles

D) Shared writing

Firefighter Zaire is preparing a report about a recent explosion. He will include the following statements in the report.

K. I quickly treated the pedestrian for the injury.

L. The explosion caused one of the glass windows in the building to shatter.

M. After the pedestrian got treated, Police Department was called to ask for help in evacuating the area.

N. After the explosion I saw a pedestrian who was bleeding from the arm.

In which of the following orders firefighter Zaire should arrange the statements in his report?

A) L, M, K, M
B) K, L, N, M
C) L, N, M, K
D) L, N, K, M

Ms. Anderson wants to teach the students transitional words and phrases like; "if...then", "as a result", and "therefore"

Which of the following composition activity will be most useful for the teacher to achieve her goal?

A) Writing a composition using descriptive or specific examples.
B) Writing a composition using sequence of events.
C) Writing a composition using cause and effect pattern.
D) Writing a composition using a list of steps.

81

What is the closest meaning of the word "federal" in the following sentence?

"DOMA was a federal law that was first enacted in 1996 by the Clinton Administration."

A) A specific law
B) The central government of a state
C) The central government of a country
D) The government and its laws

82

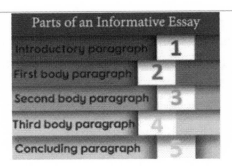

There are different types of essays; narrative, descriptive, expository, persuasive and etc. Expository essay is to educate on a certain topic.

Which of the following is a basic type of expository essay that will be easy for a reader to understand?

A) Descriptive
B) Compare and Contrast
C) Informative
D) How-to

CONTINUE ▶

83

At the beginning of the school year, a kindergarten teacher becomes aware that some students in the class have had little or no exposure to text. The teacher makes a plan to encourage students' literacy skills.

Which of the following would be the first step of the teacher while using a popular children's book?

A) To illustrate how letters of the alphabet are used to form words.

B) To demonstrate page orientation and other features such as the cover and title.

C) To point out how words are used to form sentences.

D) To show how capital letters and punctuation signal the beginning and end of sentences.

84

Which of the following terms refers to the Proficiency in reading and writing?

A) Phonics; the science of sound

B) Vocabulary; the body of words used in a specific language

C) Literacy; the ability to read and write.

D) Grammar; the system and structure of a specific language.

85

K- Convicted felons have very few rights in prison.
L- As a result, they have emotional and behavioral issues.
M- They cannot meddle with the general population outside.
N- In addition, they are isolated in their cells.

Which of the following is the correct written order of the sentences given above?

A) K-M-N-L

B) L-M-K-N

C) K-M-L-N

D) N-K-L-M

## 86

Sandra teacher presents a lesson about short vowels. She writes "_in" on the board, and wants students to offer letters to put in the blank. When students suggest a letter Sandra fills in the blank to form a new word and wants the class to read the word aloud.

Which of the following followup activities is most likely to focus on the developmental levels of all students in the class?

A) Letting students make sentences using the new words

B) Asking students to spell the new words aloud several times

C) Asking students copy the list of new words into their notebooks

D) Providing students with cut-out letters to build new words

## 87

When children learn how to use smaller muscles, like the muscles in their hands, fingers, and wrists then fine motor skills are achieved.

In a fourth grade class, which of the below would not be the teacher's best technique for encouraging the advancement of students fine motor skills?

A) Allowing children to trace the outlines of letters with color pens

B) Allowing children to participate in activities such as playing with blocks and beads

C) Involving children in drawing pictures

D) Involving children in singing song

## 88

In a shopping mall's parking lot, a distress woman approaches a duty officer and explains that two juveniles mugged her while she was walking to her car from the bank and pleaded with the officer to catch them. After listening, the officer leaves the place in pursuit of the suspects.

In the paragraph given above, which of the following words contains a grammar or spelling error?

A) Distress

B) Pleaded

C) Juveniles

D) Pursuit

Because of Chelsey's _____ attitude, many were _____ to trust her as leader of the science group.

Which of the following words accurately complete the sentence given above?

A) apathetic; compelled

B) uncaring; reluctant

C) good; unwilling

D) negative; eager

A fourth-grade teacher involves students in a brainstorming activity to identify a topic they would like to write about. The students decide to write a persuasive essay to the school board about the School Bus policy.

Which of the following is the greatest benefit of including the brainstorming activity in this lesson?

A) To increase the level of engagement among students having a difficult time mastering persuasive writing.

B) To connect persuasive writing skills to an issue that students find personally meaningful.

C) To give students an opportunity to practice persuasive writing in a content area context.

D) To help students understand the relationship between creative thinking and persuasive writing.

A language arts teacher wants to give her students the opportunity to write for an authentic audience and purpose.

Which of the following assignments would be best to achieve this goal?

A) A sympathy letter to a character in a story which is in an argument with a family member.

B) A front-page newspaper article about a true event in students' lives.

C) A letter to the school principal which states a personal opinion about a school -related issue.

D) A review of an imaginary movie from the point of view of a critic.

92

You are given the following two sentences;

"Maria saw last night the kid which delivers the morning paper."

"Last night, Maria saw the boy who delivers the morning paper."

Some corrections have been done in the second sentence. Which of the following indicates why those corrections were made?

A) Adjective placement

B) Verb agreement

C) Active voice

D) Relative pronouns

93

Consider the sentence given below.

Several restaurants continue to specialize in serving steak, and rear meats.

Which of the following indicates best if there is an English grammar problem with the sentence?

A) "Specialize" should be "specializing"

B) "Rear" should be "rare"

C) "Meats" should be "mates"

D) There are no grammar problems.

94

An **informative essay**(expository essay) aims to educate on a certain topic. It is not for giving an opinion or convincing someone to do something or change his beliefs.

Which of the following is the most basic type of informative essay?

A) How-to; provides instruction for carrying out a procedure or task.

B) Analysis; explains the significance of the text by persuading the reader of a certain point.

C) Expository; intended to explain or describe something.

D) Compare and Contrast; analyzes the differences and/or the similarities of two distinct subjects.

A teacher wants to improve her student's revision process when writing their own stories.

Which of the following should the teacher teach her students to make use of ?

A) A checklist for the revision process that would help them revise their own stories and well as their partner's stories after reading them.

B) A box-and-explode strategy in which students draw a box around a main idea in their story and then add details to expand the main idea.

C) A list of sparkle words which are more precise synonyms for the words that are most frequently used in their stories.

D) A technique for varying sentence lengths where a student highlights the end of each sentence and counts and records the total number of words in the sentence.

You are given the following sentence. Out of the options below, which one indicates best if there is an English grammar problem with it?

When you work up a sweat, you release endorphins, immediately upping your happyness levels.

A) "happyness" should be "happiness"

B) "work up" should be "workout"

C) "your" should be "you're"

D) There are no grammar problems

(1) The officer asked the inmate if something was keeping him up at night.

(2) While supervising inmates working in the facility library, an officer noticed Inmate Y was having trouble staying awake while sorting books.

(3) The officer documented what Inmate Y told him and informed the housing unit supervisor of the situation.

(4) Inmate Y replied that he and his roommate, Inmate C, were not getting along and he was worried that Inmate C might try to attack him in his sleep.

(5) Later that day, both Inmate Y and Inmate C were taken to separate holding areas for questioning.

Which of the following choices represents the most logical order for the sentences given above?

A) 2, 1, 4, 3, 5
B) 3, 2, 1, 4, 5
C) 3, 1, 5, 4, 2
D) 2, 4, 3, 5, 1

Scaffolding refers using a variety of instructional techniques to improve the understanding of students.

A teacher wishes to use scaffolding to boost student learning. Which of the following is the best example of this strategy?

A) Asking students record data they gather during classroom science experiments on the charts labeled with relevant variables.

B) Asking students to list the personal goals that they hope to achieve

C) Reviewing important information covered during recent lessons

D) Pinpointing the errors and asking them to rewrite the paragraphs correctly

Refer to the selection taken from the story *A Word in the Hand*:

"It takes two to make a quarrel," Marco told her.

"I suppose it only takes one to act like an idiot," his sister responded. "Stop it!"

"Familiarity breeds contempt," said Marco dismally. "Let's forgive and forget."

At the last part of the dialogue, which of the following does the word "contempt" mean?

A) Doubt
B) Emotion
C) Dislike
D) Anxiety

To monitor a students' writing skills progress, a teacher sets a goal of "writing a 5 sentence paragraph".

Which action below would most appropriate support this goal?

A) Evaluate the students' writing skills progress twice a year
B) Assess the students' writing skills daily
C) Evaluate the students' writing skills progress every six weeks
D) Assess the students' writing skills once a year

SECTION 6 - ENGLISH & LANGUAGE USAGE

#	Answer	Topic	Subtopic	#	Answer	Topic	Subtopic	#	Answer	Topic	Subtopic	#	Answer	Topic	Subtopic
1	A	TPRXSEB	SPRXSEB2	26	C	TK12HB	SK12HB2	51	D	TK12HB	SK12HB2	76	B	TPRXSEB	SPRXSEB2
2	D	TPRXSEB	SPRXSEB2	27	C	TPRXSEB	SPRXSEB2	52	C	TK12HB	SK12HB2	77	D	TPRXSEB	SPRXSEB2
3	B	TPRXSEB	SPRXSEB2	28	C	TK12HB	SK12HB2	53	C	TPRXSEB	SPRXSEB2	78	A	TPRXSEB	SPRXSEB2
4	B	TK12HB	SK12HB2	29	A	TK12HB	SK12HB2	54	A	TPRXSEB	SPRXSEB2	79	D	TPRXSEB	SPRXSEB2
5	A	TPRXSEB	SPRXSEB2	30	D	TPRXSEB	SPRXSEB2	55	D	TK12HB	SK12HB2	80	C	TPRXSEB	SPRXSEB2
6	A	TPRXSEB	SPRXSEB2	31	C	TPRXSEB	SPRXSEB2	56	A	TK12HB	SK12HB2	81	C	TPRXSEB	SPRXSEB2
7	C	TPRXSEB	SPRXSEB2	32	D	TPRXSEB	SPRXSEB2	57	C	TPRXSEB	SPRXSEB2	82	D	TPRXSEB	SPRXSEB2
8	D	TPRXSEB	SPRXSEB2	33	B	TK12HB	SK12HB2	58	A	TPRXSEB	SPRXSEB2	83	B	TPRXSEB	SPRXSEB2
9	B	TPRXSEB	SPRXSEB2	34	C	TK12HB	SK12HB2	59	B	TPRXSEB	SPRXSEB2	84	C	TPRXSEB	SPRXSEB2
10	D	TPRXSEB	SPRXSEB2	35	D	TPRXSEB	SPRXSEB2	60	B	TPRXSEB	SPRXSEB2	85	A	TPRXSEB	SPRXSEB2
11	C	TK12HB	SK12HB2	36	B	TPRXSEB	SPRXSEB2	61	A	TPRXSEB	SPRXSEB2	86	D	TPRXSEB	SPRXSEB2
12	C	TPRXSEB	SPRXSEB2	37	B	TK12HB	SK12HB2	62	A	TK12HB	SK12HB2	87	D	TPRXSEB	SPRXSEB2
13	D	TPRXSEB	SPRXSEB2	38	A	TK12HB	SK12HB2	63	C	TPRXSEB	SPRXSEB2	88	A	TPRXSEB	SPRXSEB2
14	A	TPRXSEB	SPRXSEB2	39	B	TPRXSEB	SPRXSEB2	64	B	TK12HB	SK12HB2	89	B	TPRXSEB	SPRXSEB2
15	D	TK12HB	SK12HB2	40	D	TK12HB	SK12HB2	65	D	TPRXSEB	SPRXSEB2	90	B	TPRXSEB	SPRXSEB2
16	A	TPRXSEB	SPRXSEB2	41	D	TPRXSEB	SPRXSEB2	66	A	TPRXSEB	SPRXSEB2	91	C	TPRXSEB	SPRXSEB2
17	D	TPRXSEB	SPRXSEB2	42	D	TPRXSEB	SPRXSEB2	67	C	TPRXSEB	SPRXSEB2	92	B	TPRXSEB	SPRXSEB2
18	A	TPRXSEB	SPRXSEB2	43	C	TPRXSEB	SPRXSEB2	68	D	TPRXSEB	SPRXSEB2	93	B	TPRXSEB	SPRXSEB2
19	A	TK12HB	SK12HB2	44	A	TPRXSEB	SPRXSEB2	69	C	TPRXSEB	SPRXSEB2	94	D	TPRXSEB	SPRXSEB2
20	D	TK12HB	SK12HB2	45	D	TPRXSEB	SPRXSEB2	70	A	TK12HB	SK12HB2	95	B	TPRXSEB	SPRXSEB2
21	D	TPRXSEB	SPRXSEB2	46	B	TPRXSEB	SPRXSEB2	71	B	TPRXSEB	SPRXSEB2	96	A	TPRXSEB	SPRXSEB2
22	A	TPRXSEB	SPRXSEB2	47	C	TPRXSEB	SPRXSEB2	72	B	TPRXSEB	SPRXSEB2	97	C	TPRXSEB	SPRXSEB2
23	B	TPRXSEB	SPRXSEB2	48	D	TPRXSEB	SPRXSEB2	73	B	TPRXSEB	SPRXSEB2	98	A	TPRXSEB	SPRXSEB2
24	A	TPRXSEB	SPRXSEB2	49	B	TK12HB	SK12HB2	74	D	TPRXSEB	SPRXSEB2	99	C	TPRXSEB	SPRXSEB2
25	B	TK12HB	SK12HB2	50	C	TPRXSEB	SPRXSEB2	75	A	TPRXSEB	SPRXSEB2	100	C	TPRXSEB	SPRXSEB2

Topics & Subtopics

Code	Description	Code	Description
SK12HB	English Language	SPRXSEB	Eglish Language Art
SK12HB2	Language Skills	SPRXSEB2	Writing

CONTINUE ▶

TEST DIRECTION

Read the questions carefully and then choose the ONE best answer to each question.

Be sure to allocate your time carefully so you are able to complete the entire test within the testing session. You may go back and review your answers at any time.

You may use any available space in your test booklet for scratch work.

Questions in this booklet are not actual test questions but they are the samples for commonly asked questions.

This test aims to cover all topics which may appear on the actual test. However some topics may not be covered.

Studying this booklet will be preparing you for the actual test. It will not guarantee improving your test score but it will help you pass your exam on the first attempt.

Some useful tips for answering multiple choice questions;

- Start with the questions that you can easily answer.

- Underline the keywords in the question.

- Be sure to read all the choices given.

- Watch for keywords such as NOT, always, only, all, never, completely.

- Do not forget to answer every question.

1

Hena wants to make a scatter plot comparing the life expectancy, represented in the y-axis, and the air pollution, given in the x-axis.

Which line fits best for Hena's expectation about her scatter plot?

A) A vertical line
B) A negative slope line
C) A positive slope line
D) A horizontal line

3

1	2	3	4	5

In the figure above, 5 parking lots are to be assigned to 5 employees; Ryan, Isabel, Mia, Giancarlo, and Cathrine. Ryan and Giancarlo are men and Isabel, Mia and Cathrine are women.

The following conditions must be met:
• Parking lot 1 is assigned to a man.
• Cathrine is assigned to Parking lot 5.
• Parking lot 4 is assigned to a woman.
• To each parking lot, a different employee must be assigned
• Mia is assigned to an odd-numbered parking lot and Ryan is assigned to an even-numbered Parking lot.

Which of the following employee may be assigned to Parking lot 3?

A) Giancarlo
B) Ryan
C) Mia
D) Cathrine

2

2, 4, 6, 8, 10, 12, 14, 16

If a number is chosen at random from the list given above, what is the probability that the number is divisible by 3?

A) 0.25
B) 0.33
C) 0.50
D) 0.75

4

From which group of letters could Jeel be selecting if it is highly likely that she will randomly select the letter A?

A) A, A, J, A, A, K
B) A, F, A, G, A, H
C) A, E, I, O, U, E
D) A, B, C, A, D, E

5

A group of 10 tourists is traveling together. Two of them are from Italy, seven are from Belgium, and one is from Japan. Among this group, two randomly selected people will gain extra benefits during their trip.

If the first person chosen is from Belgium, what is the probability that the second person will be from Italy?

A) 0.11

B) 0.20

C) 0.22

D) 0.66

6

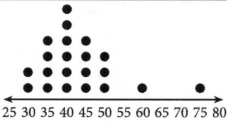

25 30 35 40 45 50 55 60 65 70 75 80
Average Flight delay (in minutes)

The average delay of flights for each of the largest 21 airline companies in Asia, was calculated and shown in the dot plot above.

If the highest flight delay is removed from the dot plot, which of the following changes occur?

A) The average will decrease only.

B) The average and median will decrease only.

C) The range and average will decrease only.

D) The median, range, and average will decrease.

7

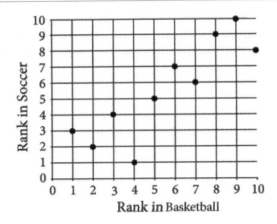

The ranking of 10 students in two sports is shown above in the scatter plot. How many students received a better rank in Soccer than Basketball?

A) 2

B) 3

C) 4

D) 5

8

A coin with two sides, heads, and tails, is flipped 4 times and the results are recorded. What is the probability that the 3rd flip results in tails?

A) 0.063

B) 0.125

C) 0.250

D) 0.500

9

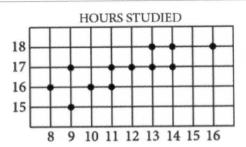

The scatter plot given above shows the number of hours, between 15 and 18, studied by 12 students of various ages, between 8 and 16, at after-school study program.

Which of the following is NOT true, according to this scatter plot?

A) More than half of the students studied more than 16 hours.

B) Four students studied exactly 17 hours.

C) One 12 years old student studied 17 hours.

D) Most of the students were over 9 years old.

155

CONTINUE ▶

10

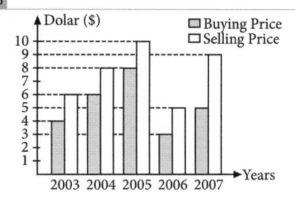

The column chart given above shows the buying and selling prices of items sold in a store between 2003 and 2007.

How many percents is the profit margin of the store in 2007?

A) 40

B) 50

C) 80

D) 90

11

DDT (dichloro-diphenyl-trichloroethane) is toxic to a wide range of animals and aquatic life, and it is suspected to cause cancer in humans. The half-life of DDT can be 20 or more years. Halflife is the amount of time it takes for half of the amount of a substance to decay. That is why the environmentalists worry about DDT because it continues to be dangerous for many years after its disposal.

If 200kg DDT has been used in a farm in 1960, how many kgs DDT will remain in 2020?

A) 25

B) 50

C) 100

D) 150

12

In 2010, the average price of a vacuuming robot was $500. In 2014, the price was $440. Based on a linear model, what is the predicted average price for 2020?

A) 20,220

B) 21,060

C) 22,680

D) 23,328

13

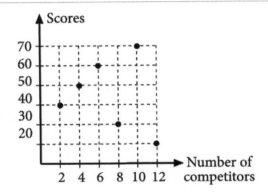

The scatter plot given above shows the sores of competitors in a performance competition. If the competitors who scored lower than 50 will be eliminated from the competition, how many competitors will be eliminated?

A) 8

B) 10

C) 20

D) 22

14

The half life of a radioactive substance is 6 days. If you have 200mg of a substabce, how many mg of it will remain after 18 days?

A) 12.5

B) 25

C) 50

D) 100

15

Each day of the month, Chad earns an allowance, in cents, equal to the square of that date of the month.

Which of the following can be the number of cents Chad could earn in a single day?

A) The mean is greater than the median, and the range is 12.

B) The median is greater than the mean, and the range is 12.

C) The median is greater than the mean, and the range is 7.

D) The mean is greater than the median, and the range is 6.

CONTINUE ▶

16

The results of the survey conducted at Montville High School indicates that the median of the heights of all of the male students was 164 centimeters and the mode was 160 centimeters.

According to this information which of the following statements must be true?

A) There are no male students taller than 164 centimeters.

B) The most frequently occurring height of the male students is 160 centimeters.

C) The average (arithmetic mean) of the heights of the male students is 162 centimeters.

D) There are more male students who are 164 centimeters tall than those who are 160 centimeters tall.

17

If the population of bacteria in a culture flask doubles every 15 minutes, the population after 1 hour and 30 minutes will be how many times the population at the start?

A) 16

B) 32

C) 64

D) 128

18

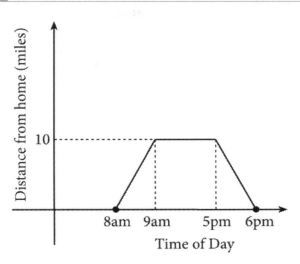

The graph above shows the distance of Sam from his home during the particular hours of a day.

Which of the expressions below can NOT be a correct information based on this graph?

A) Sam returns back to his home at 6pm.

B) Sam's Office is 10 miles away from his house.

C) Sam went to the hospital, stayed there 8 hours.

D) Between 8am and 6pm Sam stayed at home.

19

Jay kept track of the number of miles he ran each week for five weeks. The median number of miles he ran during the five weeks was 20, and the mean was 21.

Which list could show the number of miles Jay ran each of the five weeks?

A) 20, 20, 19, 18, 21
B) 24, 20, 22, 19, 20
C) 16, 17, 18, 19, 21
D) 17, 18, 19, 20, 21

20

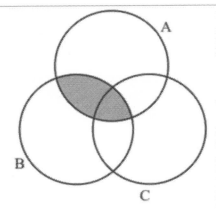

In the figure above, three circles represent single family houses on the Miami Beach. Circle A represents a house with an ocean view, Circle B represents a house with 5 bedrooms, and Circle C represents a house with a swimming pool.

What does the shaded region represent?

A) House with an ocean view, 5 bedrooms, and swimming pool
B) House with an ocean view and 5 bedrooms, but without swimming pool
C) House with an ocean view and 5 bedrooms (some possibly with swimming pool)
D) House with an ocean view and swimming pool (some possibly with 5 bedrooms)

21

In 2010, the average price of a vacuuming robot was $500. In 2014, the price was $440. Based on a linear model, what is the predicted average price for 2020?

A) 20,220

B) 21,060

C) 22,680

D) 23,328

22

In Montclair High School Mr. Alferi raised all of his students' mathematics scores on a recent exam by 12 points.

How does this increase in the scores affect the mean and the median of the scores?

A) The mean increased by 12 points, but the median remained the same.

B) The median increased by 12 points, but the mean remained the same.

C) The mean increased by 12 points, and the median increased by 12 points.

D) The mean and the median remained the same.

23

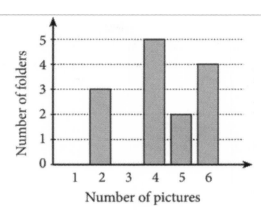

The number of pictures and folders is shown on the histogram above.

Based on this histogram, which of the following is the arithmetic mean or average of pictures per folder?

A) 4

B) 30/7

C) 60/11

D) 6

CONTINUE ▶

24

Omega 3 Content per 100 g	
X_1	0.12 mg
X_2	0.10 mg
X_3	11.44 mg
X_4	0.02 mg
X_5	9.09 mg

The data in the table above shows the average Omega 3 content per 100 grams of fish oil. Which of the following is closest to the expected amount of X3 in 20 grams of fish oil?

A) 0.024 mg
B) 0.02 mg
C) 1.818 mg
D) 2.288 mg

25

The arithmetic mean (average) of a and b is 12, and the average of c and d is 18. What is the average of a, b, c and d?

A) 3
B) 15
C) 30
D) 36

26

SCHOOL FURNITURE SETS			
Set	K	L	M
Desk	1	2	4
Chairs	6	5	2

PRICES			
Year	2002	2007	2012
Desk	$70	$80	$100
Chairs	$20	$40	$60

A school furniture company sells three sets of furnitures; set K, set L and set M. Each collection consists of a different number of tables and chairs as shown in the first table above. The second table given below the first one shows the sale prices in dollars of each table and chair in three different years.

Based on the numbers and prices given in the tables, what is the highest possible sale price in dollars of a furniture set bought in 2007?

A) $320
B) $360
C) $400
D) $420

27

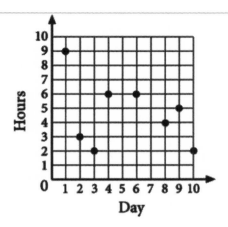

The scatterplot given above shows how many hours Eric worked for 10 days period. What is the average working hour for Eric for this 10 days period?

A) 3.6

B) 3.7

C) 4.2

D) 4.6

28

Frank will survey 25 students in his town to find out what their favorite summertime activity is. Which group would likely give the best representation for his survey?

A) 25 students at a shopping mall

B) 25 students at a library

C) 25 students taking swimming lessons

D) 25 students in his school

29

In a survey of a random sample of 1,500 residents aged 30 years or older from Essex County in New Jersey, 600 residents had a bachelor's degree or higher.

If the entire Essex county had 720,000 residents aged 30 years or older, around how many county residents would be expected to have a bachelor's degree or higher?

A) 288,000

B) 320,000

C) 360,000

D) 432,000

30

Buses from two different bus routes each stop at the same corner at 10 A.M. Buses from one route stop at that corner every 9 minutes. Buses from the other route stop there every 12 minutes.

What is the fewest number of minutes that will pass until the next time buses from both routes are at that corner at the same time?

A) 108 minutes

B) 54 minutes

C) 36 minutes

D) 21 minutes

31

A publishing company is going to have 32,000 books printed. There are between three and four books out of every 4,000 printed that will have a printing error.

At this rate, which number could be the exact number of books that will have a printing error?

A) 23

B) 30

C) 33

D) 42

32

Alyssa biked 2.82 miles on Monday, 3.75 miles on Wednesday, and 2.13 miles on Friday. Alyssa estimated the total distance she biked.

Which of the following statements correctly compares an estimate of the total distance with the exact total distance that Alyssa biked?

A) The estimate $3 + 4 + 2$ is nearly 1 mile greater than the exact answer.

B) The estimate $3 + 4 + 2$ is nearly 1 mile smaller than the exact answer.

C) The estimate $2 + 4 + 2$ is nearly 1 mile greater than the exact answer.

D) The estimate $2 + 4 + 2$ is nearly 1 mile smaller than the exact answer.

33

Inmate	Assignment	Time
Adrian	Kitchen	1:30 p.m. – 3:00 p.m.
Nader	Library	1:00 p.m. – 4:30 p.m.
Roger	Infirmary	1:30 p.m. – 3:30 p.m.
Luis	Gym	1:15 p.m. – 3:45 p.m.
Marcus	Laundry	2:00 p.m. – 4:00 p.m.

Which inmate is available at 1:30 in the afternoon for a 15-minute meeting with the correction officer based on the assignments given in the table above?

A) Luis

B) Marcus

C) Adrian

D) Nader

34

Sullivan creates a scatter plot with a negative association. The x-axis of the scatter plot is titled, "Minutes Spent at Shopping Mall".

Which label is most likely the title of the y-axis of Sullivan's scatter plot?

A) Number of Stores Visited

B) Number of Movies Seen

C) Money Available to Spend

D) Distance Walked

35

Laundry Schedule

Time	Inmate Group	Duration
9:05 a.m.	Group K	35 minutes
9:45 a.m.	Group L	45 minutes
10:25 a.m.	Group M	40 minutes
11:30 a.m.	Group N	35 minutes
12:10 p.m.	Group O	55 minutes

The table above shows the the laundry schedule for the day in a facillity.

Which of the following two groups have library times that overlap with each other?

A) Group K and L

B) Group L and M

C) Group M and N

D) Group N and O

36

In an Escape Room, one of the games entails finding the combinations to a lock to open a safe and find the clue inside.

How many valid combinations exist for the lock if it has four 0-9 digits?

A) 10000

B) 1000

C) 90000

D) 9000

37

Movie Theatre Attendance

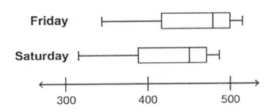

A movie theater kept track of the attendance on Fridays and Saturdays. The results are shown in the box plots above.

Which conclusion can be drawn from the box plots?

A) The attendance on Friday has a greater median than attendance on Saturday, but both data sets have the same interquartile range.

B) The attendance on Friday has a greater interquartile range than attendance on Saturday, but both data sets have the same median.

C) The attendance on Friday has a greater median and a greater interquartile range than attendance on Saturday.

D) The attendance on Friday and the attendance on Saturday have the same median and interquartile range.

38

The average of eight numbers in a list is 56. If one of the numbers is removed from the list, the new average becomes 44.

Which of the following is the number that is removed?

A) 12
B) 90
C) 96
D) 140

39

Alicia is a student at Ridgewood High School. She surveyed a random sample of the sophomore class of his high school to determine whether the Spring Festival should be held in April or May. Of the 80 students surveyed, 30% preferred April and the rest preferred May.

According to this information, about how many students in the entire 240 person class would be expected to prefer having the Spring Festival in May?

A) 56

B) 72

C) 96

D) 168

40

Fire Department Report					
Company	Number of Trucks	Total Number of Calls Received	Total Number of Calls Dispatched	Number of Fire Calls Worked	Number of False Alarms
A	3	101	90	60	12
B	2	99	85	58	7
C	5	412	274	198	22
D	4	110	72	56	13
E	7	623	428	212	109
F	6	519	275	168	33
G	4	228	102	69	18

Which of the following is the average number of trucks for companies that dispatched more than 100 calls?

A) 6.2

B) 5.4

C) 5.2

D) 4.8

SECTION 7 - MATH - PROBLEMS & DATA ANALYSIS

#	Answer	Topic	Subtopic	#	Answer	Topic	Subtopic	#	Answer	Topic	Subtopic	#	Answer	Topic	Subtopic
1	B	TB	S3	11	A	TB	S3	21	D	TB	S3	31	B	TB	S3
2	A	TB	S3	12	D	TB	S3	22	C	TB	S3	32	A	TB	S3
3	C	TB	S3	13	D	TB	S3	23	B	TB	S3	33	B	TB	S3
4	A	TB	S3	14	B	TB	S3	24	D	TB	S3	34	C	TB	S3
5	C	TB	S3	15	D	TB	S3	25	B	TB	S3	35	B	TB	S3
6	C	TB	S3	16	B	TB	S3	26	C	TB	S3	36	A	TB	S3
7	D	TB	S3	17	C	TB	S3	27	B	TB	S3	37	A	TB	S3
8	D	TB	S3	18	D	TB	S3	28	D	TB	S3	38	D	TB	S3
9	B	TB	S3	19	B	TB	S3	29	A	TB	S3	39	D	TB	S3
10	C	TB	S3	20	C	TB	S3	30	C	TB	S3	40	C	TB	S3

Topics & Subtopics

Code	Description	Code	Description
SB3	Problem Solving and Data Analysis	TB	Mathematics

CONTINUE ▶

Made in the USA
Coppell, TX
14 January 2021